Catholic Worker Houses

Ordinary Miracles

Sheila Durkin Dierks
Patricia Powers Ladley

Sheed & Ward

For PHD who first saw the miracles and Peter who opened up the world of
the Catholic Worker.

Scripture references taken from the New American Bible.

Photography by Sheila Dierks

Copyright © 1988
Sheila Dierks
Patricia Ladley

Sheed & Ward™ is a service of National Catholic Reporter Publishing Company, Inc.

Library of Congress Catalog Card Number: 87-62910

ISBN: 1-55612-109-1

Published by: Sheed & Ward
                115 E. Armour Blvd., P.O. Box 414292
                Kansas City, MO 64141-4292

To order, call: 800-333-7373

Contents

Prologue

This book is a celebration!

It celebrates the Catholic Worker Movement. It celebrates the thousands of persons who voluntarily live the Beatitudes (Mt. 5ff) and the Works of Mercy (Mt. 25) in hard places. It looks at the Catholic Worker Movement through the eyes of several houses of hospitality who share their lived experience, and speak the miracles they have known.

Some thirty Catholic Worker Houses, chosen for their diversity and accessibility, were invited to participate with us in this reflection on the miracle of the Movement. Almost half responded; and half of this number welcomed our visit. Over the course of about eighteen months, we lived and worked with the volunteers and guests in each of the houses portrayed in this book. We ate, and drank, laughed and cried, worked and prayed, and listened. We offered each community the opportunity to reflect on its own story.

The chapters which follow are not our stories, but those of the guests and volunteers who people these Catholic Worker communities. They are true stories. They are the evidence of miracles in our midst today.

Yes, miracles, real ones, happen every day. These miracles take place in the weariest parts of town, places where the rents are lowest, the crime worst, the drugs most available, the dropout rate highest. Often they occur in the midst of sadness, mental illness, and heartbreak.

These are the miracles of the Catholic Worker Movement, the "haves" sit at table with the "have nots," the "cast-offs" of our society serve one another, strangers are welcomed without fear or ridicule, the Works of Mercy replace the works of war, every person is received as sister or brother. These are the real miracles. They are not uncommon; they are experienced daily. They are the loaves and fishes of Jesus multiplied in our time.

This book, these stories, invite all of us to open our hearts and to dare to experience miracles. Perhaps we shall discover, in spite of the horrors of our times, the truth of Jesus' words, "...whoever believes in me will perform the same words as I do myself, he will perform even greater works..." (Jn. 14:12).

Scott/Harris Catholic Worker House of Hospitality

Washington, D.C.

There is an old house on T Street, a house on the edge of ruin. The floors slant precariously, the ceilings bow, the windows reveal, as the light passes through, an amazing amount of dirt. The storage on the drooping front porch is a fire marshall's nightmare. The original quality of the plaster is perversely displayed by the thick edges where holes have been knocked in the walls. Residents and visitors are constantly accompanied by the fragrance of sauerkraut. This is the Scott/Harris Catholic Worker House of Hospitality.

The story of this house began shortly after Christmas 1978. Michael Kirwan was working on a master's degree in sociology at George Washington University and living in a small apartment on campus. He says: "I was out walking one bitterly cold night and happened to come across a homeless man living on a heating vent near the State Department. I hurried past him, embarrassed to look, but I heard him call after me. I was annoyed, but I stopped and he asked me for a dollar to buy a cup of soup. I didn't believe him and anyway I didn't have a dollar, but his disappointment moved me and I told him I would fix a bowl of soup in my apartment and bring it out to him. I did, with a jug of water and a couple of pieces of bread. I never saw him again, but that night I kept thinking about him. The next night I went out again just to see if he was there. He wasn't, but someone else was, and this time without a word I went back and fixed more soup and bread and tea. I brought it down and walked away. And that was how it all began."

Mike is a big, handsome Irishman with silver-flecked dark hair. He seems out of place in cords and a flannel shirt: his appearance is more suited to banker-gray pinstripes. He has the physical presence of a young politician coupled with the look of solidity favored by corporate attorneys.

"After the first six months one of the men asked to come up to my apartment to clean up and shave. I told him no. I was embarrassed by him—dirty, unkempt and awful smelling. I had friends; it was campus housing and my apartment was filled with "valu-ables" like a stereo, books, etcetera. But he persisted, and the next night I said yes, but he would have to leave right away and could only shower and shave. He stayed 30 days and did not budge from the apartment. He was afraid that if he left I wouldn't let him back in. I used to come home from work and find dinner cooked, the apartment immaculate, and my guest sitting there listening to Wagner. He looked wonderful! It was living with him, who had looked so repulsive on the street, so dirty and unkempt, so smelly and unattractive, even fearful-looking, that first opened my eyes to the fact that men and women anywhere, under any circumstances, are always and foremost human beings with the same needs of love, respect and most of all the desire to be wanted. I realized in this man—my first understanding of what Dorothy had for so many years been talking about—that we are indeed our brothers' and sisters' keeper, and we must love even if that love is the most difficult of loves, for in the end that love is all that matters."

Interesting words from a man who had known the Catholic Worker philosophy all his life, who had grown up on a Worker farm in Virginia, who had known Dorothy Day well, whose parents were close to her. The experience of conversion, of revelation, came only in his adult years.

"I don't think that Glen's story had a happy ending, but I'm not sure. I gave him a key to the apartment after the first 30 days, and he went out and got drunk. I found him in an alley in the pouring rain, and I literally dragged him home. He stayed again for a long time, but one day he left and I never saw him again. Even those who regularly saw him had no explanation. But by the time he left, I had 15 other homeless men in my apartment. He had opened my heart, and I trusted and loved them all. When the university officials discovered my community of homeless men, they were shocked and ordered me to get rid of everyone. The bottom line was that I could stay but not with the men. Since I refused to do that, I was forced to find another place to live. That is how I came to found our first house of hospitality."

Michael was experiencing exactly what Dorothy Day had encounted many years before. She wrote:

No one asked us to do this work. The mayor of the city did not come along and ask us to run a bread line or a hospice to supplement the municipal lodging house. Nor did the Bishop or Cardinal ask that we help out the Catholic Charities in their endeavor to help the poor. No one asked us to start an agency or an institution of any kind. On our responsibility, because we are our brother's keeper, because of a sense of personal responsibility, we began to try to see Christ in each one that came to us. If a man came in hungry, there was always something in the ice box, if he needed a bed and we were crowded, there was always a quarter around to buy a bed on the Bowery. If he needed clothes, there were our friends to be appealed to, after we had taken the extra coat out of the closet first, of course. It might be someone else's coat but that was all right, too (*Meditations,* p. 66).

There is an old house on T Street. It is a red three-story brick building called home by 40 men and a few women who have come in from the streets of Washington. Alma came with the house. She was living there when Mike made the purchase. He couldn't bear to evict her.

No one is turned away though the house is bursting. One must step very carefully after 10 p.m. to avoid sleeping men. The long front hall, lit only with a dim bulb, is lined with filled sleeping bags, as are the kitchen, dining room and every other square inch of available floor space. Only the stairs remain clear. Transient guests take possession of the first floor; staying a while can result in a space upstairs, maybe even a bed, and a small, jealously guarded area to stow worldly goods. Among the long-termers are Pete and Judy, a married couple with a room of their own. There is Ulyses (sic), a published playwright and poet and self-described "black Hemingway," whose life got off the track after two bouts in prison. There is Rory and his son Ralph, a teenager, who is very interested in all that a free-footed life has to offer. Rory, a frustrated monk, says of their residence, "We are seeking community and a life of prayer."

For all it is a place under cover, out of the weather, simple and safe from assault and hunger and more of a home than anyplace they've been in a long, long time.

In the February 1959 issue of *The Catholic Worker,* Dorothy wrote:

Within *The Catholic Worker,* there has

always been such emphasis placed on the works of mercy, feeding the hungry, clothing the naked, sheltering the harborless, that it has seemed to many of our intellectuals a top heavy performance. There was early criticism that we were taking on 'rotten lumber that would sink a ship.' 'Derelict' was the term used most often. As though Jesus did not come to live with the lost, to save the lost, to show them the way. His love was always shown most tenderly to the poor, the derelict, the prodigal son, so that he would leave the ninety-nine just ones to go after the one.

Her thoughts are given flesh among the blacks, whites, refugees, the elderly, the addicts, the winos and the handicapped who find their way to the house of hospitality. One could say that a community of wounded persons dwells here, hospitality seekers who, because of the pressure of necessity, become hospitality givers.

Michael, for all his great energy, good-humor and patience, can be stretched only so far, and so the guests take over first small jobs, then bigger responsibilities. In the stacking of canned food, in the answering of the phone, in the washing of dishes, ministry to others begins. Respect grows.

The house has two rules. Number one: No one can bring liquor into the house. Number two: Michael doesn't call the police. They have both been broken, but not often, and with lessened frequency as the residents pa-

trol themselves. Either rule breached is a threat to the whole community, and everyone knows it.

Since no one else in the city serves an evening meal, Scott/Harris House tries to fill the bellies. Sweeney, wearing a billed cap which proclaims "I'm good at EVERYTHING I do" over his braided gray hair, cooks for 100 guests a day. He wants to even though it means hobbling around on a leg broken in four places. (He thinks he got hit by a car.) Ulyses frets that Sweeney is doing too much. He fusses after him, drying plates, sweeping and straightening.

In another lifetime Ray was an air traffic controller. That was before President Reagan settled the air traffic controllers' strike by firing everyone. Ray ended up on the grates, but now has come in and gradually taken over much of the day-to-day running of the house. Michael says "You just can't imagine how grateful I am to him. He eases things so." And Ray does have an easy smile and a manner which turns aside a lot of trouble waiting to happen.

Ray needs some time off now, he's fragile still, and there are other men willing to come forward, willing to shoulder a bit of the job. Society may have written them off, may see them as faceless and threatening, but here they know they are trusted, their labor valued. Willingness and smiles are signatures of mealtime. And yet, for all the goodness of this little community, there is not one who would remain if offered a cleaner, quieter, more private place to dwell.

Dorothy said in May 1984;

It is a wonder... . They do not go away.... But "bad as we are, it is worse outside," someone said, or "Though I am unhappy here, I am more unhappy elsewhere," someone else said. And so we are really...a community of need, a community of "wounded ones." ...I myself have often thought of our communities as concentration camps of displaced people, all of whom want community, but at the same time want privacy, a little log cabin of their own, to grow their own food.

There is no better hospitality than the hospitality of the poor. They have known so much need themselves; they recognize the needs of others. So the house on T Street reaches out.

Every evening, after those who come to dine have departed, a simple supper is carried to the grates. These grates surround government buildings and vent excess heat, an unexpected Federal surplus.

Michael packs a blue plastic milk crate full of hotdogs on hamburger buns. ("Should we let them put the catsup and mustard on or should we put it on here?") There's a big jar of the ubiquitous sauerkraut, a jug of water and small jars of soup. Men dressed for the cold in knot caps, parkas, jeans or camouflage pants, boots, emerge from the shadows of the shrubbery to stand on the main grate just off Virginia Avenue.

No one talks much; there is no pushing. An odd, almost Southern courtesy is in force. They are hungry though, and there is a palpable air of unwilling control. Fat Tony, Wolfman, Blue, Leroy, Darrell, Quiet Willy, Jack, Ella, the only woman in the assembly, Herman, Cotton-top and Max all join in this communal picnic. It is a travesty of the American ideal of alfresco dining, since the temperature is working hard to get below 20 degrees. Soup is put by for a friend too drunk at this moment to get off his grate.

Though the house survives on donations and Michael literally does not often know the source of the next meal, he insists that it is important to stretch to feed the residents of the grates. That service of food is a reminder to the house community: I am my brothers' and sisters' keeper; even I have a bit to share. As Dorothy Day commented 50 years ago:

The disciples didn't know our Lord on that weary walk to Emmaus until He sat down and ate with them. "They knew Him in the breaking of bread." And how many loaves of bread are we breaking with our hungry fellows these days—13,500 or so in this last month. Help us to do this work, help us to know each other in the breaking of bread! In knowing each other, in knowing the least of His children, we are knowing Him (By Little and By Little, pp. 80-81).

Michael Kirwan is a most curious man. He is an odd combination of humor and sadness, wholeness and brokenness, capability and inefficiency. He can take $50 to Murry's Meats (an all-purpose cheap food store) and

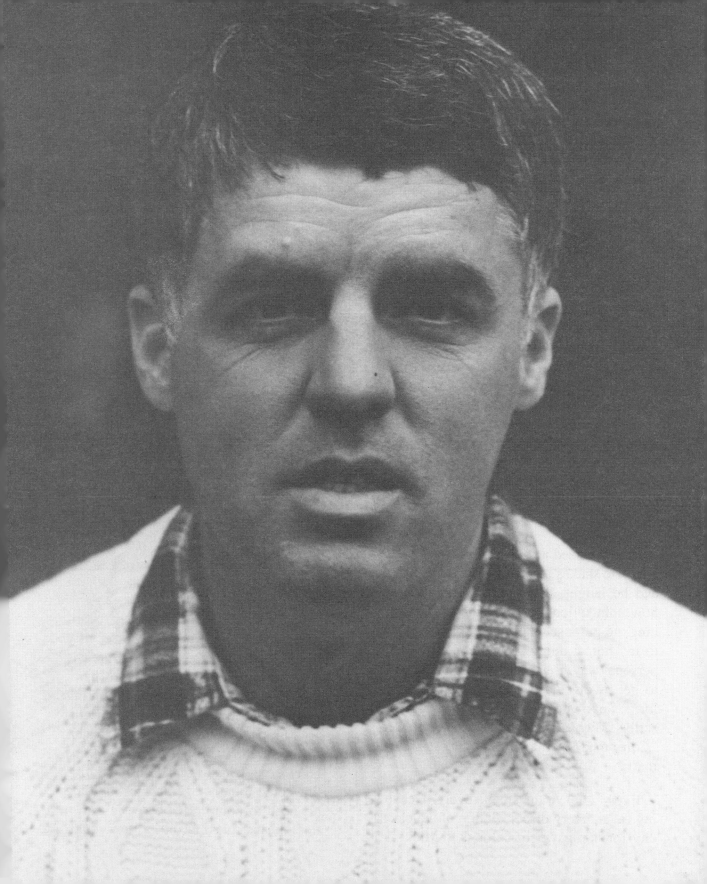

brutally squeeze every nickel into three nights' worth of dinner but go softhearted and buy catsup, a luxury item, "because the men love it so much." He can sweet talk the car repair man into doing a vital fixup, but can't convince the bank that he will *absolutely* never overdraw again. He is childlike in his gratitude for every contribution, without restraint in thanks. There is a nakedness, as if all the acquired emotional constraints of society are peeled back and he has no defense against the bare need of others. There is simple evidence that he is chronically unable to say no to a request; witness the fact that he owns only the clothes which currently cover him—a white sweater, brown cords and a badly faded flannel shirt. In cruel January! "I did have a coat before Christmas, but there was this woman on the grates. She was lying there in a summer dress and no shoes. I went over, but she started to scream so I just dropped the coat and ran."

He is amazed at how all this has come to pass. He shakes his head, his eyes crinkle up and he laughs, "How small this all began, how unintentional. No forethought, no planning, no purpose other than taking people into my home; doing what I could in a small personal way. It was never ever my intention to get involved, to start houses of hospitality." "Involved" does not adequately describe Michael; neither does "immersed." "Consumed" perhaps comes closest to the mark.

Every unpleasant smell, every overflowing toilet, every disconnection of the electricity for non-payment belongs to Michael as it does to every soul in the house; so does every success, every job won, every triumph of the poor over the system, every joke.

Michael has a way of being there that is not forced, not dominating, but comfortable, gentle, honest. "I don't want to foster dependency. They look to me as a parent, but I try not to look at them as children...more as family." Michael has come to expect little and he demands nothing. "If I sit down for dinner and have forgotten a cup, and someone sees that and gets me one, I can live on that show of love all day."

Much is demanded of him: coping with the Vietnam nightmares of the one man which erupt with terrifying regularity in time of darkness and rend the sleeping air; dealing in kindness and without reproach with a regular who has discovered, to his amazement, a massive infestation of lice; breaking down the bathroom door in fear of a suicide within.

In the September 1983 issue of *The Catholic Worker* Dorothy Day wrote,

Our poverty is not a stark and dreary poverty, because we have the security which living together brings. But it is that living together that is often hard. Beds crowded together, much coming and going, people sleeping on the floor, no bathing facilities, only cold water. These are the hardships. Poverty means body lice. A man fainted on the coffee line some months ago and just holding his head to pour coffee between drawn lips means picking up a few bugs.

Poverty means lack of soap and Lysol and cleaning powders.

What fuels Michael? What keeps him in this place when it is obvious that he could easily practice law, be in government service, perhaps still serving the poor, but at least going home to a clean bed every evening, to the pleasures of a good meal, to a night out with friends?

There is a long pause; Michael considers. It is a conundrum often pondered. What are his reasons? "I read *The Long Loneliness* (Dorothy Day's autobiography). I knew that was the way to go. It was correct. I wasn't a biblical scholar, but I knew Dorothy Day was correct. To see the gospels enacted makes them come alive."

The gospels lived fully call for choices, small and large deaths to self, some easier, some more painful, and Michael has had more than his portion. He was forced to choose between ordination and the men; he saw an engagement go awry under the pressure of this call; and the daily need and poverty have slowly but surely subtracted from his existence every worldly possession. A poignant sight is the headboard and footboard of a bed-that-used-to-be, leaning against the wall of his bedroom\office, the mattress only a memory. A bedroll is neat on the floor.

"Yes, there are real moments of doubt and despair, but we've got to keep forgiving. I love them; they love me. Hope is the final virtue. These men need to know that it isn't the end of the line, that someone still loves

them, still believes in them." Michael believes, but on occasion with slumped shoulders.

The house on T Street courts disaster, and there is a miracle quality about waking up every morning to find that it, and its inhabitants, have survived to face another day.

Michael goes shopping with all the money in the house, about $100. Careful, intensely careful buying yields food for 40 people—ten big cans of baked beans, packs of turkey franks, and a product called "pork chopettes" which the box describes as "scraped and reformed meat product." A better name is mystery meat, but it is protein, an item in perilously short supply. Next stop is Zayer's, a discount shoppers' paradise. Here Michael looks in vain for a pair of size 12 1/2 work boots for one of the men. None exists. There is some laughter, wry humor, concerning people with feet that large needing specialized services the house cannot provide. Michael settles for size 12; the feet will be covered if somewhat cramped. He flattens his wallet in the process. He is worried. The food can be stretched for a couple of days, but he and the house are now broke. Returning home he finds the mail yields up two checks, one for $10 from a regular contributor and a surprise of $250 from someone he does not know. His face lights up; his eyes form exclamation points. The following morning a an unexpected delivery of surplus food from Amtrak appears. These are nice groceries—crossants stuffed with meat, good apples, Granny Smiths. Michael bites down on that cold, tart, crisp sweetness and remarks, "This is my favorite kind of apple,

and, my goodness, my goodness, this solves the food problem." As he surveys the bounty, he says, "I am so blessed to be able to take part in these miracles. Nothing ever comes until you really need it, and then just enough, only just enough. Yes it comes, but not without cost. And why not?"

This business is all consuming, taking in the homeless, listening to their struggles, sorting out their bickerings. Michael has to escape sometimes and he does, to his mother's apartment where he tries to catch up on sleep and wash his clothes. He also makes a trip to the Pentagon daily. He goes to walk the five sides and say the Rosary, always the Sorrowful Mysteries, one decade per side. The mysteries remind him of the pain of Jesus. "I began when I realized that there are lots of demonstrations on the feast of the Holy Innocents, or on the anniversary of Hiroshima, but no one is here on a daily basis."

The days are gray and damp and on the sharp side in January. The walk leads from the vast parking lot down one long side pierced endlessly by the same tiny windows, definitely a fortress. The angle made, he moves past a long row of bus shelters. Now he prays the second mystery, The Scourging at the Pillar, as he passes rows of covered bays named endlessly for the destinations of the buses, pointing to the reality that Pentagon workers foraged from every suburb of Maryland and Virginia, almost to Baltimore,

earn their daily bread at this font of nuclear planning.

Finally he arrives at the colonaded front portico. It is impressive, powerful, imperial. The central six columns are cleaner, whiter that the rest, a reminder of their regular sandblasting to remove the blood splashed on them by those who resist the unthinkable destruction contained within.

In the October 1940 issue of *The Catholic Worker* Dorothy Day wrote:

There are so many who hate war and who are opposed to peace time conscription who do not know what they can do, who have no sense of united effort, and who will sit back and accept with resignation the evils which are imposed upon us. This is not working for God's will to be done on earth as it is in heaven. This is accepting the evils in the world as inevitable and looking toward heaven as a haven, a "pie in the sky" attitude. God did not make the evils, but man in the misuse of his free will.

And, daily, Michael goes back to the old house on T Street, back home to a family of outsiders. It is a home to which each one brings his own gifts and his own broken self. Some can do nothing except provide the others with an opportunity to love, and here that is enough.

Unity Acres

Syracuse, New York

The fields themselves seem to have fallen on hard times. In the early spring the plows have not attended to them, and they lie uncared for. There is no hope of prosperity, no promise of this year's crop in them.

Many of the homes, houses of weather beaten, unpainted clapboard, tell the same story. Barns are picturesque to the casual glance but closer scrutiny reveals outbuildings with caving roofs and barn doors loose on hinges. The occasional bright silo is a surprise.

In this area of high unemployment, where even the farms offer little in the way of sustenance, is Unity Acres. It appears as a cluster of six or eight white wooden buildings huddled together near the edge of County Road #2. It is more than this though; it is home, home to more than 100 men who have lived the hard life on the streets of Syracuse, in prisons and institutions. Leo, one-time professional organist who plays at daily liturgy, lives here. So does the old black man in his 80's who "takes care of everybody." There are the elderly long-term residents and the young men who wash out and find a temporary home until they gain the courage to try again.

The structure and furnishings of this once-abandoned sanitarium are simple—in bold contrast to the richness of spirit, of love, which dwells in the people who live here. Hercule Thibault is an example. Ten years ago Herc gave up his store in Syracuse and moved to Unity Acres as a volunteer. He speaks not of himself, nor of his service, but of the self-sacrifice of others. "My sister got me here. What she was doing when the men were housed in the city...cleaning up after they got sick, washing the sheets... . I realized I had a car and could help with the men, get them out of town, get them out for a while." Herc, it is said, "just serves and serves the men." His response, his rock-bottom line, is "What would Christ have done?"

Herc points to Kate Stanton. "Kate's another one, so faithful!" Kate is a stocky, graying woman who has been with the Catholic Worker Movement since the first house was opened in Syracuse in 1966. She hadn't intended to get involved when she met Father Ray McVey who was already ministering to the poor at St. Lucy's, an inner-city parish. With his encouragement she soon found herself mothering approximately twenty guests with drug and alcohol addictions in the cramped quarters of that first house. When they left the city for the space and health of the country, Kate came too.

"I feel good about it after 19 years. Before, I worked in a factory and I hurt my back; I couldn't do the job. The Lord took care of me. I didn't want to join the Legion of Mary (at St. Lucy's) because I don't like to go places alone. I went to one or two meetings, then Father Ray got me! I had such a void; I was searching and didn't know it. The longer I stay, the better I feel... . I felt like I'd never done anything in my life, but when I came here I realized I'd spent all my time getting ready for it."

This doesn't mean that life at Unity Acres is pure bliss. "Once a man comes, you really kind of make a commitment to him." Because the farm is 38 miles from Syracuse and because of the deteriorated condition of many of the guests from years of abuse, long drives are frequently necessary to obtain good medical treatment. In addition, Kate and Father Ray spend more hours than there are in a day in overseeing finances, dispensing prescribed drugs, answering the phone, celebrating Mass and welcoming newcomers. And listening, listening constantly to the needs of the men, listening to their stories, their woes, their pain and joy.

Father Ray speaks about how he handles the thousands of demands on him, "I've decided never to make a schedule or a plan; it just never works. I do what I have to do at the moment and don't worry about the rest." His weekly day off is Monday when he rises early to get some reading done and then, on a busman's holiday, goes to Syracuse to visit guests who are in hospitals and nursing homes.

One of the miracles of this place is that in the midst of such ever-present need Father Ray and Kate are full of laughter, an easy humor that signals faithful acceptance of the unexpected and sometimes bizarre in their hectic lives.

Kate has come to Unity Acres, and she has stayed "to share their joy and sorrow." To her each one of the men is an individual whom she tries to accept as he is. "It's hard for me at times. I'm working on it, not putting conditions on it, but sometimes that's difficult."

Father Ray is a small man, dressed in a sweatshirt and washpants that have seen more than their fair share of wearing. He looks more a member of this little community than he does a parish priest. He is dressed for the labors which surround him. A great consumer of black coffee, he is also a smoker of handrolled cigarettes. In his face and manner there is the selflessness sometimes found in mothers of large families, a visible, palpable living for others. It is as if he has forgotten that he ever had needs of his own.

Father Ray credits Tony Walsh of Benedict Labre House in Montreal with being "God's instrument of grace" for him in the early years of his priesthood. Tony's influence led him into ministry to and ultimately living with "our wounded, broken, and isolated brothers and sisters." The loving arms of Dorothy Day and the Catholic Worker Movement were discovered later. Kate made several trips to New York City to talk with Dorothy. Both she and Father Ray were impressed with how thoroughly her philosophy coincided with theirs. "We were struck with the simplicity of the whole thing, the idea of not being tied to a bureaucracy, just simply serving the gospel." When Dorothy was presented with the idea of the farm she said, "You're a fool; it will never work." But later, on one of her visits, she remarked, "How many times I wanted to bite my tongue for what I said to you."

Father Ray remembers the beginnings of this "foolish" community. Unity Corner, a center for teens at St. Lucy's was the first endeavor. Then, for $2,500 a house of hospitality was purchased. The first guest was a heroin abuser. That home was open to whatever needs could be served. "Soon we were inundated with men. We had bunks three tiers high in the living room. A drunk in the top bunk fell out and broke his hip. He was so quiet about it that we didn't even know until morning."

"We had nothing worked out financially, but we had 30 men there. So I called Carol and Jerry Berrigan and told them we were hungry." They responded immediately by

forming teams from their parish who arrived to cook, serve and eat with the guests.

But even with the overflowing kindness of many, the city with its temptations of alcohol, drugs and violence became more than Father Ray could handle. "I needed to flee and invited the men to come with me."

"We offered the owner of a tuberculosis sanitarium, abandoned since 1958, the sum of $18,000. We didn't have the money. A priest friend took out a loan for $7,000 and we bought up the mortgage."

So Unity Acres began. Five men went from the city with Father Ray, and soon the number increased to 65. "Then we were at 210 fast." Families with children were among the early residents, but the mix became too difficult and the decision was made to house men only. Houses and trailers were gradually purchased so the families could stay in the area. Even today families from the area are welcome to offer Sunday liturgy and stay for dinner.

With so many in residence, providing for the daily needs of food, clothing and heat is an act of faith in God's providence. And these needs are miraculously met by the generosity of faithful souls who regularly send donations.

The men are not asked to share in the expenses of their upkeep even though many of them receive a small Social Security check. However, it soon became obvious that many were spending their money for alcohol obtained on visits to Syracuse. Both Kate and Father Ray came separately to the conclusion that this was a real problem. They approached the men with an idea. Would anyone be willing to contribute half of his checks, not for Unity Acres but for Mother Teresa in India? Many agreed, and the men take great delight in their ability to help others. And, as Kate says, "We haven't wanted for anything since we began to send it to her."

Who is it that calls forth such a heartening response from this group of damaged individuals? Some of the men respond: "Father McVey is the biggest drawing card—selfless." "Father is a saint. At one time we had 11 murderers here and Father talked to them.... It's a miracle that there is no violence."

"Wild Man" Don, long time resident, hermit, carpenter, builder of waterfalls, comments: "I was so mean. My hair hung all the way down my back. I was on the streets of Syracuse about six months when my parole officer brought me up here. What turned me around? Kate and Father. They talked to me. Took a long time, but they turned me around."

Father Ray returns the compliment, "Don, you are one of our miracles."

There are other miracles, too, many of which flow from Father Ray's sensitivity to the humanity of each of the men. He lifts up their goodness and allows them to minister to each other. Carlos is a good example.

Carlos came to Unity Acres knowing not a word of English. He spent much of his time, in bad humor and isolated, muttering to himself in Spanish. "One of the guys knew a little Spanish and latched onto Carlos," breaking down his defenses and drawing him out. "He got Carlos working in the canteen and interested in fishing. Now Carlos is really happy and gets along well with the others. His whole life is the canteen and fishing."

Shorty is another miracle story. In 1970 his social worker pleaded for help. Abandoned as a baby on Randall's Island, Shorty had lived 49 years in a state school. Released, his next step might have been prison. Father Ray and Kate took him in. "I treat him like my son," Father Ray says. "He's a gem. He'll do anything." And he does. From serving daily Mass to flower gardening, from running errands to being a committee of one, welcoming guests, his eagerness is a gift.

Shorty's happiness was made complete about five years ago when a social worker and a computer teamed up to find his long-lost family. The many years of loneliness were ended, miraculously, on Holy Saturday when the pair unearthed not one relative, as Shorty had hoped for, but 26, a resurrection of the family he had never known. Shorty knows he is one of the blessed ones. His brothers and sister, nieces and nephews have lovingly received him. Proudly he displays their photographs in his tiny room, "Come in and see my family."

With quiet enthusiasm, Father Ray mirrors back the essential beauty of Shorty and the other men whom society fears and shuns. Here they find space, freedom from pressure, the opportunity to open up, a chance to rediscover their identities.

"I have hidden from myself," writes Bartley, in a poem titled "The Journey." He is a younger man, passionately Irish, and feels impelled by the Spirit to be a writer. A long and difficult road from childhood Catholicism through atheism, Eastern mysticism, and communism led to a conversion moment in November, of 1980. Bart, now firmly returned to the Catholic church, has experienced a gradual healing of the spirit at Unity Acres. Today he says, "Yes, I'm home now, I've entered into His rest." Simultaneously, he has been able to reach out to his brothers in trouble.

Father Ray says, "He is genuine, good with the men; he tries to touch those the church is not reaching. You can see the fruits; he is a very spiritual man."

I...
know eternity to be serenity
know serenity to be achieved
only by lessening the pain of others.
I will continue,
surely I will continue

from "The Journey"

Will Unity Acres continue? Father Ray says, "There was a lot of spirit with the men in the growing years. That spirit is hard to maintain. We don't have recreation programs, but they all get on so well. We

need people, volunteers, to build the spirit here. A lot of little things need to be done. So many are old and sick.... It's important for the men to feel needed; they need to work. The Lord will provide. He'll provide the right people and we'll go on."

Unity Acres is many things: a good meal, a room of one's own, a breathing space in the midst of life's storms, a home. Here the poor become more than a burden, or challenge, or object of service. Here each one who comes is a student in the school of love. This is where Joe tends his pigs with pride and eagerly shares his newly acquired knowledge of animal husbandry. Here Shorty furrows the earth to create patterns of color and beauty with flower and shrub. Here Leo coaxes intensely sweet music from a relic organ, and three or four outdoorsmen make harmony with saw and tree. "They care," says Helen Clark, community cook and perpetual baker of birthday cakes. "They look out for each other. They are beautiful out here!"

The guests, like the fields which surround them, have fallen on hard times. Yet these men are full of promise, for love is asowing in Unity Acres.

St. Martin de Porres

San Francisco, California

It is a week before Thanksgiving, and Carol, Charlie and Barbara lounge around ramshackle desks discussing the shopping list for the holiday dinner.

25 turkeys
60 pounds of macaroni
a case of celery
4 cases of lettuce
120 dozen eggs
600 sweet rolls
50 pounds of ham
100 loaves of San Francisco's
best sourdough bread

a case of red peppers
50 gallons of milk
coffee to make 120 gallons
15 cases of oranges
17 cartons of cigarettes
dessert—as much as we can beg

The shopping list is massive, but then so is the guest list. At St. Martin de Porres Catholic Worker House 600 people will arrive for the feast. No one will be turned away; everyone will have seconds or thirds. The groceries will not be purchased, but they will come—such is the faith of these three. The groceries always arrive because they must. They have a family to nourish.

This story is an oft-lived one at Martin's a 15-year-old soup kitchen in the once elegant, then fallen, now yuppie-haven gingerbread glory of San Francisco's Potrero District.

Approximately 15,000 people a month sit down to dine at Martin's, and no bill is presented at the end of the meal. It is picked up through the kindness of those who send checks monthly, who deliver bread or beans or fruit or meat, who come to serve and leave some cash.

Jack, a meal-crew chief, comments, "The first day I came to work we were low of bread. I could just tell we were going to run out. I ran around frantic, but just as we ran out a truck pulled up from a bakery and started unloading bread, and it was still warm! I said, 'You guys set me up for this!' But it wasn't a setup, and I've come to accept it as normal. If there's something we need, we get it; it just comes. If it doesn't come, we don't need it."

Larry Galla, a priest who lives as a layman, is a balding, attractive soul with a Thomas Merton face. Having worked at Martin's for years he says, "The miracle that I see and which touches me is that there's tons of food, good food, out there, and people need to eat. Here it is done." His smile arches his eyebrows upward. "A miracle is that we *never* run out of food, never. Many times we have thought we would be short, but it comes in, always."

The guests, family, of Martin's are the confluence of many human rivers: those who came to the Golden Gate in the height of the hippie movement in the late '60's and early '70's and discovered a life of drugs was not easy to escape; those who come now, many from the cold Northeast or the bitter winters of the Plains states and find that there is no work or that their skills are not sufficient. Losers, drifters, Vietnam vets who can't get over the nightmares, gays with AIDS or paralyzed by the fear of it. Many are young, some even well-dressed. Many carry books which they devour while standing in line for lunch. Alistair MacLean is popular; so is Dick Francis. An occasional volume of Tolstoi or Twain is visible.

A good-looking, big-eared man named Sonny leans against a post. He is in his 20's, wears a navy windbreaker and packs a copy of *A Connecticut Yankee in King Arthur's Court*. A bookmark is about halfway through. "The book was free. I got it from the book box (a carton of used paperbacks

available to all). Sometimes the people who sit around me aren't the greatest conversationalists, so I always bring a book."

Readers or not, varied though their backgrounds may be, the guests of Martin's express over and over the comfort they feel here. John, a stocky black man in his '50's who sports a grizzled beard remarks, "I can go to (he names another soup kitchen in the area) hungry and come out hungry, but no one lines you up here, no one feed you water soup. This place is what it's all about. You can come here and don't speak the language but you can understand what going down here."

Tall, lean, badly marked from years on the streets, Harry is a walking mismatch, a reminder of the fact that he wears his whole wardrobe. "This is no Salvation Army. You don't have to listen to the sermon before they feed you. Hell, their food ain't worth it anyway. But here, these folks just love you and feed you and the food is damn good! I used to eat in restaurants, and there's food I paid for not as good as this."

The volunteers who staff the shifts (breakfast daily and lunch every day except Monday) are as assorted a crew as the guests.

Alison Ulman, a sculptor, pauses from bread slicing, pushing a long strand of golden hair into the safety of a red bandanna. "I came here after a long search. You see, I am technically disabled. I've got an old person living in a young person's body, and I needed something to do to get outside myself. I heard someone talking on TV about

hunger, and Martin's seemed so direct. It was a joy to come here. It's a raw situation, raw soul here. There is undisguised love on the gut level. I like how they approach people; it's so human and unpretentious. There's no fear. People who come are asking and in need. The miracles happen because we need them."

Scooping "Iran Scam" bean soup from a bottomless pot for the endless line is Robert Cole, astrologer, former seminarian, author of *The Book of Houses*. He chuckles at his route to the door of Martin's. "I was arrested on April Fool's Day while marching in the St. Stupid's Day Parade (a San Francisco tradition). I was trying to defend an old woman who had been flattened by a cop, so I slugged him. I was sentenced to 16 hours of community service and chose this place, and I've been here on the Wednesday lunch shift ever since." He gently wipes a dribble from the lip of a soup bowl before handing it, with a grin, to a young black man who smiles in return. "Hands Across America really revitalized this place. People started thinking again about the problem of hunger. The Catholic Worker is special; I think it is the North American branch of liberation theology. It's anti-government, which is great since government is no solution. In fact, it's the problem. We have an option here at the end of the '80's. We can take the Catholic Worker Movement, the liberation theology movement and present a new left, not a Communist Left but a radical liberal Left after the fashion of Dorothy Day." Robert pushes his glasses back up the bridge of his nose and meticulously tidies the serving counter. The pervading sentiment here is that just because the family is poor is no justification for sloppiness.

"When I don't come, I miss it." John De Lois, a potter from Maine who now teaches ceramics in several places, including the San Bruno County jail, is giving backrubs at the end of the shift. The crackle of vertibrae and sighs of relief indicate that he has talent in more than one area. "I like the people who come and the people who work. Two years ago on Thanksgiving I filled in for someone and felt at home, so I just keep coming back."

John also gives time in a local hospice and does massage therapy for AIDS patients who are being transfused.

If Martin's attracts the young, the hip, the counter-cultural, it is also magnet to the older, the mainliners.

"My wife died last year, and I just didn't know what to do with myself after that. I did start volunteering, passing out bed tickets at Old St. Mary's. But I heard about this place." George, prossessor of the bluest eyes and whitest hair on the property, works slowly and carefully in the back room. He is cutting desserts and cleaning up. At 72 he has a sort of Santa Claus appearance, lacking the whiskers. "They asked me here if I was used to hard work, hard kitchen work, and I figured that was something I could do." George scrapes tiny niblets of fudge frosting from the table as he talks. "This place gives me a feeling of satisfaction. It helps others, but it helps me more. You get in with young people here. I am amazed by the variety of

people who are guests and the variety who are workers." Looking around in wonder, "So many well educated!"

Sitting on a milk carton in the storage area is Max Magen, a skeleton earring bobbing from one ear. When he gets excited, the bones bounce. He is exchanging soup recipes with John of the Berkeley Catholic Worker. John, new to the soup game, is having problems with beans burning on the pot bottom before the soup is ready. Max makes one or two suggestions which may cut down on kettle scrubbing, and they move on to discuss spices and herbs, the merits of celery seed in the split pea and how much garlic should be used per gallon. The philosophical implications of the vegetarian pot are considered. (Martin's always has one, and even has the sensitivity to keep separate stirrers and ladles.)

Max is a piece of work. Dressed in black, he wears his curly hair collar long but with the sides above the ears very short, almost punk, but not quite. With a grin on his cherub face he certainly does not give the impression, at 26, of a man with a rap sheet which is reaching book size.

Max, whose given name is Peter, began life as the son of a successful, liberal Jewish family in Philadelphia. In his early teens a beloved older brother died, and Max turned to drugs. By the age of 19 he found politics, especially the politics of a nuclear age, and deciding they were more fun than pot, he began a life of non-violent anti-nuclear protest. Max has impeccable credentials in the movement, with a background in the Clam-

shell Alliance, at Rocky Flats and Diablo Canyon. He has frequently been civilly disobedient in protest of United States nuclear policy and has been arrested and jailed "maybe 20 times" for his actions. He sees all this as absolutely necessary because of his religious credo. A declared pagan, he calls himself a witch and worships Mother Earth. "How can I let them pollute and destroy her?"

Max learned the art of cooking for crowds when faced with huge numbers and the limitations of a campfire at anti-nuke rallies and camps. It is a skill which serves him well today. After moving to San Francisco in 1985 Max started helping out at Martin's. When he began he was "totally blissed out by the experience." He muses, "Martin's fits in comfortably with my political philosophy. This society needs to be changed radically, but on the day after the revolution Martin's will be open... to serve the needs of the individual."

Leaping from his perch, he rushes to hug a young woman who has entered bearing a donation of bread. Arms and loaves entwine as they embrace. "People who haven't experienced this kind of place think I'm doing something wonderful, but I get so much; it heals me. I get to go on and deal with my life because of what I get here. I love to be able to share, I didn't buy it but I sure cooked. It is great to be able to give seconds, to 'spoil' people. Places like Martin's prove that there is enough for all of us, enough food, enough love."

Most delightful of the volunteers is 83-year-old Mary Catherine Mulligan. Tiny, white-haired and slightly bent with age, she sits high on a stool setting cookies on a tray for lunch and pursuing an intensely political topic with an aproned young woman. They are in delighted radical agreement. Mary has been an integral member of the Thursday team since 1978.

"I was volunteering for Women For Peace, doing filing in the office, when I came across Martin's newsletter. It made me think about my brother Irwin. We were living in Columbus, Ohio, in the 1930s and Irwin would get drunk and go on a binge and he wouldn't come home. But he would go to be fed at a soup kitchen at St. Francis Hospital there. I was always grateful to them for what they gave him." Mary pauses and nibbles a chocolate chip cookie. "Irwin died in 1938." And so, a seed that was planted in the '30's has grown and borne fruit in the '80's as Mary Mulligan does for others what others did for her brother decades ago and 2000 miles away.

Martin's seems to call forth the very best from its volunteers, eliciting an intensity of dedication in the face of others' helplessness, a spirit of sharing with those who have less, a gift of love when confronted with weakness, disease, lice and mental disrepair. And who is it that organizes, encourages and provides the backbone for this house of hope?

Carol Arete is dressed in bluejeans, a red plaid shirt and glorious striped suspenders. Perhaps 40, she looks strong, with a sturdy body and crisp salt-and-pepper hair. She is quietly everywhere, on the phone chatting up a possible donor, on tiptoe on an upturned milk carton to stir the soup, arms round a guest hugging a greeting, softly in a corner with a young vagrant who is hungry but afraid to come forward.

Carol lives above the kitchen; her quarters can best be called monastic spare. It is difficult for her to discuss in depth her five years of immersion here, but her emotions are rich. "Coming to Martin's is the best thing that ever happened to me in my life. I can't think of anything I'd rather do. I am grateful for meaningful work and this is the most meaningful. Sometimes I don't leave here for a week at a time except to go to Mass. It took me so many years to find my destiny I don't need to spend time anywhere else. I might take a couple hours once in a while, but no real vacations. Some people go to a psychiatrist one place, and have a job another place and a community they go to somewhere else, but I've got it all in one place."

Carol's patience with drunken guests and new volunteers is unceasing. In the midst of a very busy lunch, Timmy, a frequent diner, arrived happy and drunk in a taxicab. He entered, waving his bottle. Carol cheerfully escorted him back outside. He soon re-entered, this time with the bottle in a brown sack. Still good humored, Carol linked arms with Timmy and together they went out and sat regally in the back seat of the Yellow Cab where Timmy and the driver were treated to bowls of Martin's turkey barley soup. The driver asked for seconds.

Carol is one of the very few to have any connection with the Catholic church. She admits tremendous diversity of belief among volunteers, many of whom object to the "Catholic" in Catholic Worker or, at least, to the capitalization of the word. "People here are vehemently anti-church but are loaded with spirituality. Everyone, the Zens, the pagans, the Jews, seems to be on the same path regardless of what word they use for God."

The variety of people who give service does not surprise Carol. "Food is not a privilege. It is a right, and people of all denominations who know that deep inside themselves come here to work. When we serve lunch the important thing about the person next to you behind the counter isn't where, or if, he or she goes to church; the important thing is recognizing the dignity of every member of our family who needs a bowl of soup and some bread and fruit."

Charlie Ingelstein lives that recognition. Charlie once tried to get a job as a counsellor in a half-way house. Fully qualified he was nonetheless rejected as "too empathic, does not see need for distance between client and counsellor."

He is a full-time member of the unpaid staff, a man come home to a place where all available empathy is in demand. A Jew from New York, the son of a postal worker, he says, "I read about the Catholic Worker and said yes; I came not knowing much about the Catholic Worker Movement, but there is a lot I basically agree with. I am an anarchist; I won't cooperate with the government

and refuse to vote, like Dorothy Day. I see Christ as one of the great teachers."

Charlie looks perpetually tired, but he is always moving, knee twitching, finger popping, on the phone. There is an intensity in his lean bluejeaned frame, a quickness of movement which leads one to theorize that Charlie's mental list is never completely checked off. The rumor is that once Charlie worked Wall Street, but his efforts are in carpentry now, carpentry and reconciliation and service.

"I see myself in the (soup) line more than as a worker. I'm more like them, closer to them than I am to the people who come to work, and then go home. My needs are few. Jeans out of the donations, a pair of shoes, maybe once a year." Charlie observes the sneakered foot cocked on his knee, "Maybe the year is up this week. I learned to repair cars, and I buy secondhand. But it's difficult to live in America and not live in contradiction. Everything you do can be abusive to someone else, so I try to live simply and to maintain a consciousness about others' needs. The material world is seductive. I have chosen that my life is and will be different." His smile is gentle, almost apologetic. "I'll never work a 40 hour week. I carry no insurance. If something happens someone will take care of me." Charlie fiddles with his glasses, a piece of scotch tape binds once side into wholeness. "There are no special ministries here; for example, lots of guys with AIDS come in, but we don't say we have a special ministry to them because it would diminish other needs. AIDS people are lepers; society mostly wants to discard them, but they are comfortable here because there aren't any labels. No, you are just a human being here; there is no separation."

Charlie's words are proven out on both sides of the serving counter with gays, lesbians and straights both distributing and receiving. One handsome young gay man, Jack, came to work, met David, a crew chief, the man who became his lover. When David died of AIDS the community of Martin's congregated to bid him farewell at the funeral Mass and Jack's loving tribute was to take on David's job in command of a shift.

Charlie's gentle leadership and Carol's dependable steadiness are the perfect foils for Barbara Collier's effervescent charisma. She is glitter and splash in this sometimes colorless setting. Barbara is high profile, a vividly-spoken lavender butterfly. Always garbed in shades of purple, a wardrobe gathered from the donation pile which on her is high fashion, with a sparkly trail of earrings up each lobe, she is the most visible member of the trio that guides the house.

Barbara has had a long and fascinating journey to Martin's, has been here quite a while and certainly intends to stay. She, like Charlie, began life as a child of Russian Jews, but her Bohemian parents did not practice their faith and she was heavily influenced by her grandfather who had a kosher butchershop in Los Angeles. On Friday afternoons before he shuttered the shop for the Sabbath, he would give away his unsold meat to the poor. "He was considered a fool, not a hustler," says Barbara, "but he still touches me. You don't hoard; you share what you've got."

A large Mexican Catholic family whose daughter was Barbara's best childhood friend became part of her life. She was enchanted by the shrines which filled their home, and there she discovered Jesus. Their influence encouraged her to "do something for Jesus" during Lent and to find a spot at daily Mass by the time she reached 12. Skipping college, Barbara went to Israel for two years of kibbutz life and found there that she "walked where Jesus walked." Smoothing back her silver hair, Barbara recalls, "He spoke to me. He made so much sense. I got his message. When I was growing up I learned the great prayer, 'I will love the Lord my God with all my heart and all my soul and my neighbor as myself.' Then I discovered Jesus who told me just a few ways to do what was commanded." Barbara absolutely jiggles with excitement, her voice full of exclamation points. "I'm having a love affair with God. He sent Jesus with a few little rules to put love into effect! Wow! He tells us to feed, to clothe, to shelter. Now *what* could be simpler than that?" She flings her arms in the air; 40 silver bracelets jingle. "Fifteen years ago I was back in California, deep in the hippie movement, and I was reading the New York *Catholic Worker*. I saw an ad for help at the San Francisco Catholic Worker. They wanted someone to cook, so I started there and pretty soon I 'owned' it!" Sometimes the whole experience is daunting for Barbara, but her faith, her willingness to do the work, shoulder the yoke is vivid.

The phone rings and Barbara swivels toward it. "Hello....oh, hello.... You've got 20 bushels of potatoes? Great!... Well, how moldy are they?.... Let's put it this way, would you feed them to your family?... Well, I guess we wouldn't feed them to our family either."

Cradling the receiver, she arches her eyebrows, "This is my family here. I want them to eat as well as any family can eat. It's an insult to them and to Jesus to expect that just because they're poor they'll be happy with anything."

Up from the desk Barbara rushes to the door where milk is being brought in. She hugs and kisses the delivery man and sorts the problem of storage, which involves rotating the older milk forward in the cooler so that nothing will be wasted. Returning from dairy detail she spots, with the practiced eye of a long-term volunteer, that a disagreement is brewing between men who await soup. In a flash she is among them, speaking their names, making a joke, cleansing the air, calming the feelings. Grinning, back at the desk, she says, "The greatest gift I've been given is the opportunity to serve, being able to love without limit. Oh, it's always been tested, but my heart almost breaks with the abundance of love here."

Barbara has been the most visible public figure in what has become a major miracle in blasé San Francisco. Although Martin's is 15 years old, it was not always housed on Potrero Street. Bob Morse wrote in his December 20, 1985, column in the San Francisco *Examiner*:

For fifteen years Martin de Porres House of Hospitality was the unknown soup kitchen, at least to the general public, if not to the hundreds of needy people who dine there. Suddenly the friendly little Mission soup kitchen is becoming well-known but not for the best of reasons. It is being evicted from its present quarters, and that has become a news story. The staff of Martin's is not exactly pleased with having TV crews and reporters tramping through their dining room and disturbing their extended family even though the publicity may help them raise the $300,000 they will need to buy new quarters. The lease runs out in three months, and they need $40,000 up front very quickly as a downpayment on a nearby property.... I asked (Barbara) Collier what they will do if they fail to come up with enough money for a new home. "We will," she said simply and powerfully. I believed her. For 10 years, this electrically energetic woman has cooked for about 400 people a day. That's a track record.

At the time of the article Barbara had no real idea where they would go. "People told me we'd never find a new building, but this is when we get our faith," she grins triumphantly. "We decided we could. We had no money but we raised $500,000 fast. You know, faith comes in when you are down to your last penny. I just said to myself, 'Don't whine; just get in there and do it!'"

Carol comments, "No one would rent to us if they knew what we were doing. We knew that we would have to buy. We started looking at places in the $175,000-200,000 range. They were totally inappropriate, and anyway, we didn't have that kind of money. Then a guest told us about this place." She smiles at the memory.

In the May issue of *Sequoia,* Ann Scott chronicled their progress.

A perfect place—a former bakery-turned-autobody shop—has been found in the commercial district just a few blocks away on Potrero at 15th. The spacious building has all the ingredients needed to be a home for Martin's brand of hospitality: a sheltered, off-the-street area for guests to wait in line, lots of electricity, dry storage areas. But it carries a steep price tag: $700,000 to buy and restore. Since no residential area wants a soup kitchen in its midst, Martin's volunteers have decided that the only possible home they will be able to find in the Mission, where they're so needed, will be in a commercial area. They also want to buy, rather than rent, because it's safer. Several years ago to meet City health codes, Martin's had to put $30,000 of work into its present location, including a new roof. Now they must leave it behind.

"After months of searching, this new building has been found," says Barbara, who reports that more miracles have already brought the soup kitchen $142,000 of the immediately needed $200,000 down payment. "There must be lots of others out there who are just dying to help us out," she says, ever-optimistically. "They just have to know about us." The record says she is right.

And right, right, right, she was!

Carol still looks amazed, "People began to send in checks for $1,000; people who had never heard of us sent money. One check for $40,000 came from a woman who had always had a devotion to St. Martin de Porres!"

But even as the bank account mounted toward the magic number needed for the purchase, other difficulties developed. Opposition to the establishment of a soup kitchen at the new address bloomed. A group titled "Potrero Hill Betterment Society" and one named "Potrero Hill Boosters" decided to fight the granting of necessary permits, fearing that the presence of Martin's would mean a swelling of litter, traffic and crime statistics.

"Our guests have always been in this area," Charlie insists. "It's just that the poor and the homeless are invisible to many people. They just tend to look through them and step over them, until something like this comes along."

In July the San Francisco Planning Commission listed the permit review on its agenda, and the folks of Martin's turned out in style. One hundred and fifty guests, servers and financial supporters packed the commission's hearing room, armed with brown bag lunches direct from the kitchen. They even arrived with food sufficient for the commissioners' mid-day meal.

Testimony for the adversaries stressed worries about upward spiralling violence, which was countered by State Assemblyman, Art Agnos, whose investigation had shown no crime increase in Martin's current location over a 15-year period. Distress about possible litter got a sharp response from Barbara who shot back, "We'll put out extra garbage cans. We'll clean the whole neighborhood. We'll clean the whole city."

Mayor Diane Feinstein sent an endorsement to be read and Jim Herman, president of the International Longshoremen's and Warehousemen's Union spoke of the long tradition of hospitality in the neighborhood. "Potrero Hill is a neighborhood of poor and working people. Many of us who live there have, at various times in our lives, wondered where the next meal was coming from. We recognize the Martin de Porres clientele as part of our community, with legitimate needs that we must somehow seek to fill."

In the August issue of *The Potrero View*, Stephanie Potter told the outcome,

As a crowd of supporters whooped in delight, the Martin de Porres House of Hospitality won its latest battle for survival last month when the city's Planning Commission voted unanimously to approve permit applications for the soup kitchen's newly purchased building.

Delight and rejoicing filled up that small hearing room. Guests hugged volunteers, commissioners hugged guests, opponents embraced. Jawbreaker grins were seen all around as the final step in the miracle took place.

Larry Galla has fond remembrances. "This experience of moving into a new place is a miracle. People worried a lot. I said, 'We can only do so much. God has to do his or her part.' And God does! It is a miracle!" Looking back over that worrisome time, Larry becomes bemused. "Everyone knew someone who was helpful. It's been a series of miracles. The people who supported us before the Planning Commission, the columnists who supported us publicly. God provides. The miracle is in the goodwill and the good intentions of good people. Our strength is in our weakness. We call forth the real caring of others." His eyebrows arch up behind his hornrim glasses as he smiles.

And so it is the morning of Thanksgiving. The sun warms the long courtyard of the autobody shop turned soup kitchen. The temperature is friendly, and workers are comfortable in sweats as they rush toward completion of the midday meal. Breakfast has already been served to 600, and the same number will arrive for lunch. Enormous pots of turkey with pasta bubble, men and women slice loaf after endless loaf of crusty sourdough bread which is then carefully tented with plastic to avoid dryness. For the occasion Barbara sports an earring crafted from a turkey wishbone. When asked, she points out that the statue of St. Martin in the dining room wears a necklace of the same. "For

many years we had barley and onions. Then turkeys started coming in. These turkeys gave their lives and the wishbones are the symbols of this gift. We keep them because they're like relics to us. They sacrificed so that we could eat, could live."

In the storage area, rows and rows of folding tables have been erected to receive the bounty of desserts, and volunteers nibble—"Just to make sure they're good"—as they cut pans of brownies and pumpkin pies and carrot cakes. The day before, four carloads of students and teachers from St. John Ursuline High School had been honored by the local meter maids with $40 tickets for double-parking while delivering sweets.

The family begins to come, by ones and twos, as the hour of the feast approaches. Workers still tear greens for salad. In the balmy courtyard, on benches created from boards nailed to plastic milk cartons, hungry men, women, children pass the time. The atmosphere is party-like.

Today will be special, no one will stand in line, each will be escorted to a seat where he or she will be served. The guests love it. So do the workers. As seating begins the courtyard takes on the air of a smart restaurant. One volunteer acts as maitre d' and a guest jokes, "There are five of us, and we'd like a table on the terrace with a good view."

The atmosphere is definitely family. Barbara, Charlie and Carol are constantly on the floor, kissing and hugging and greeting old friends who wouldn't dream of going anywhere else for their Thanksgiving meal.

There is a wonderful mix of people. American Indians, welcome but surprising presences, take a round table. There are many Orientals, a share of blacks and whites. One strikingly beautiful woman leaning on a cane shows up on the arm of a toothless gentleman wearing a cache of campaign buttons on his jacket. One young man comes in but cannot celebrate; he is thoroughly strung out on drugs. Barbara sits with him on a bench for over an hour, wiping his face and embracing him as he is consumed by a narcotic-induced delirium.

Everyone is delighted with the food. Many have seconds, and coffee is poured again and again. "This is my best Thanksgiving in years!" "No one looks down on us here." "There's no regimentation." "I'm so full I can barely walk!" "Can I get a plate to go? My ol' lady's sick at home and can't come in. I think she'd like a piece of the lemon pie... or maybe that chocolate cake there."

And with all this, they are offered a sack of sandwiches and fruit and cookies to take away for the evening. "All this and a bag to go? I can't believe it," giggles one guest.

The shopping list has been filled. The turkeys and the celery and the bread and the dessert have appeared, been prepared and consumed. The massive effort is over. The workers congratulate themselves because Martin's has survived with style its first Thanksgiving in the new house. They are tired and jubilant and tomorrow morning Charlie and Carol and Barbara will be back, making coffee, stirring the soup and slicing the bread.

Holy Family House

Kansas City, Missouri

It is a misty summertime morning. The sun is struggling behind a morass of charcoal clouds. Gray drizzle triumphs and offers its gift to the upturned faces of dahlias, petunias and nicotinia which populate the beds edging the porches of the two residences which comprise Holy Family House.

The houses sit together on a slight rise, pleasant companions, like two old ladies who cling when all others their age have died. On the north side of 31st Street, in the

900 block, the other homes have yielded to the destruction phase of redevelopment.

The Holy Family houses are ample and sturdy, dependable providers of food to many and shelter to women and children. Three stories of dressed stone, stained glass, oak woodwork and floors are signs of quality. The solidity suggests a neighborhood different from the one presented now. Across the street is the Silver Leaf Tavern, advertising Coors, hip to thigh with the Imperial Cleaners which flashes a two-hour service sign. A parking lot comes next, for bar patrons, but few have cars and mostly it belongs to Crazy Wino Joe who has squatter's rights and feeds the birds. Vacant lots alternate with boarded store fronts. Some are still in business, but all plate glass has fallen victim to the need to deny easy access to the till.

The front doors of the two Holy Family houses open almost simultaneously, and by ones and twos men and women emerge, six in all, staff and volunteers. It is 6:45 a.m. and they are on their way to Mass at St. James Catholic Church.

Marlys Graettinger has the key in the ignition. The car is old and resents the call to perform in the rain. Moving away, the occupants are quiet, the windshield wipers' rhythmic swish a whisper.

They kneel together, Brother Louis Rodemann, Thomas Allgaier, Marlys, Sister Jan Cebula, Sister Teresa Horn-Bostel and Dennis Coday. They kneel to celebrate the Eucharist, a sacrament lived out daily in the reality of Jesus present in those at the door and in bread broken and shared at the nightly table.

Breakfast is a mildly communal matter. By 7:45 a.m. the worshippers have returned. The coffeepot has bubbled its dark magic, and those remaining at home have gathered in the kitchen. The group is subdued. Maybe it's the weather, maybe the nature of morning metabolism. Most of the staff are on their way to work. In order to sustain the house, everyone is employed half- to-three-quarter-time. Brother Louis has a Solzhenitsyn face and head and the tanned and muscled hands and arms of a farm worker. An intriguing combination because Louis daily bends his back to the load and yet his mind is one of a quiet prophet. He will soon depart for Seton Center, a neighborhood gathering space which provides services to elderly and to the poor. He teaches basic skills to illiterates.

"Education is a goal, a strategy," he comments while pouring milk on his cereal, "a move toward improvement; reading a clock, reading a letter, not getting screwed out of money because they can't read." He peers through his glasses into the spoon drawer. "There is a woman who thinks she's about 65 who's learned to read to the third grade level and now she can do basic math problems. That isn't great, but it's a miracle because she came from no skills at all."

Lack of literacy is only one of the problems this community endures; another is homelessness. "I suppose you make a distinction between those who are visibly

homeless, perhaps 500, and many times more than that who are homeless but less visible because of temporary shelter. That kind of shelter can be municipal or given by family or friends. You see, there's a widespread strategy on the part of city development to make downtown 'nice.' What used to be low or moderate rent housing has been converted or torn down. It makes it hard for people who live on benefits."

And the poverty. He continues, "I listen, but there is a big gap between the experience of being totally poor and listening sympathetically to the stories of pain and need. No one chooses that life. I can easily imagine living with a lot less than I have. For me total poverty would be not having a community. We have levels of community here. First, there is the community of staff, those of us who live in the house. Then there is the more open community of staff and volunteers; finally the wider circle of staff, volunteers and guests. Each circle is so important and has so much to give."

Louis smiles his slow smile, "Where I really see poverty in my life is in a lack of space and time. Oh, for a few minutes to be quiet, not to answer the door or the phone, a place to be quiet. After five years here I'm still not good at making space and time. I go too fast too long, then the need becomes exagerated. Jan tells me to slow down, but I'm hard of hearing. Yes, I'm efficient, but I'd love more time to be with guests, not on a job basis, but just as friends."

One part of Louis's life which has fallen victim to the strictures of time is political demonstration. Though arrested in the past for anti-war protest, he now is more centered on the needs of the house. Three weeks in Guatemala recently helped to remind him of what a political gesture the very existence of the house is. "In Guatemala people are being shot for exactly the kinds of ministries we perform here."

Sister Teresa, sporting a "Farms Not Arms" T-shirt, is examining the contents of the refrigerator. She will depart soon for St. Therese Little Flower parish, an inner-city church which employs her in social ministry. She joined the convent at 17 and spent years teaching in St. Louis. When her parents' health worsened in 1982 and she saw an ad asking for summer help at Holy Family she returned to Kansas City. Though both parents are now dead she has not left.

Sister Teresa is a forceful woman. Daily she labors for the poor and her anger at the economic system which stifles so many flares, a well-fed inner fire. "There are so many families now, so many children who weren't on the streets before. I see it at work and I see it here. Why, just the diaper phenomenon! Five years ago we didn't hand out diapers. Now we can go through a case a day. They're absolutely necessary. How are you going to wash diapers if you've got a baby and nowhere to live?" Sparks fly. "In the last month here we've had three mothers with two to four children each whom we've put up. They have *nowhere* else to go. Oh, those poor children, dragged from one place to another. How can anyone expect them to grow up healthy?" Teresa shakes her head, not a gentle shake; it snaps back and forth.

"It helps so much to be in a place like this. The funding (all contributions) is a miracle. We have yet to want. We can answer needs without red tape, so we can be generous with anyone who asks. It's always there. The miracle is that you have what you need. That's phenomenal!"

Teresa's voice is an exclamation point, her excitement brightens the kitchen, the sun emerges. "It continues everywhere we go. We have enough to be able to give $1000 a month to St. James where they do the paperwork for rent assistance. We stay committed to hospitality and feeding. These are our focus. We spend about $500 a month on food, and there's a tremendous gift of stores; bakery stuff and vegetables. On Saturdays we go dumpster diving."

Dumpster diving is a Holy Family House sport conducted at the outdoor city market. It involves arriving in midafternoon as many of the farmers are closing for the day. Volunteers and staff invade the dumpsters searching for usable food, discarded because of bruises or blemishes which do not affect taste or nutrition. The previous Saturday's booty included half a dozen beautiful watermelons, slightly cracked; several crates of peaches, badly in need of sorting; 30 or 40 perfect cucumbers; twice that number of zucchini; 50 pounds of perfect golden carrots donated by a merchant friend of Louis'; numerous cantaloupe; and a half case of tomatoes. The small miracle came in the final dumpster. On top of trash and decay lay 20 dozen sweetheart roses in a crayon box of colors: pinks, fuschias, reds, yellows, apricots, white. Packaged for sale in quantities of a dozen, the outer petals had been brown-tipped by frost, their only blemish. A few moments of judicious plucking would ready them for the dinner tables.

Teresa's grin flashes, "Dumpster diving keeps us in touch with those who are poor. It keeps fresh vegetables on the table in greater quantity than we could afford. It reminds us of our beginnings. And bless the volunteers! We have people who come on Saturdays just to sort, peel, pit and pack the food we find in garbage dumps." Teresa smiles, rinses her bowl, spoon and mug and leaves for work.

The house was born in 1974, called into life by a need for education and consciousness-raising on tax and draft resistance. Vietnam was still a mountainous debacle. The infrequency of street living called for few physical survival resources.

1980 brought Cubans for whom the house served as a temporary way station. It was not until 1981, however, that recongnition of shifting needs signaled the debut of a soup kitchen. The first meal fed 20 people.

Now the demands for full-day services are enormous, and the staff dreams of a member who can remain at home and meet those needs. Marlys, a primary-school teacher, has filled those shoes for the summer.

It is almost 9:00 a.m. The doorbell peals the first of the day's demands. The 31st Street grapevine has carried the news that the house has tennis shoes, new white leather ones. A whole case.

"You all giving out shoes today? I take a size eight." The man's face folds into a frown when he discovers their largest is seven and a half. He is only momentarily daunted. "I'll take them anyway. I'll just cut the toes out!" Marlys, and Thomas, a summer volunteer, play shoe store all morning.

In one strikingly beautiful moment, Thomas kneels before a young black girl, perhaps 6 years old, and gently washes her feet, one at a time, drying them tenderly, before finding new shoes to fit.

The phone's bell punctuates the morning. Sister Carie Novitzke and Nettie, young summer volunteers, are pressed into service.

"Can you help me get away from here? I've been living with my boy friend and he's beating on me. I'm sure my parents will take me back. Can I get bus fare? I'm desperate."

"I just got a letter from Welfare says my check's going to be cut off."

"We have a woman down here who needs a place to stay. Do you have space?"

By lunch time a caller at the back door has delivered several crates of lush emerald broccoli, cucumbers and robust heads of cabbage, treats from the garden. There is such abundance that much will be served for dinner and more will be frozen.

Noon brings the unexpected and delicious gift of a few moment's respite. Marlys discovers left-over salad lurking behind the margarine in the back of the refrigerator and settles in the dining room, one of three which will fill this evening. For now it is an oasis of cool and quiet. "Four years ago I spent a month here through Shared Horizons, a volunteer program. At the time I was teaching in Iowa and doing some personal searching. In the month I was here some questions in my life came into focus."

This is an Iowa farm woman. No frail bloom, she is tall, strong and capable. She is equal to demanding work. Marlys returned in August 1984 to stay.

"I'm the only staff member who hasn't been in religious community. I welcomed the life, but it took a while to adjust, to figure out how to live intimately with other adults." With cheerful emphasis, she adds, "It's been a growthful thing."

"We pray together on Sunday and Tuesday nights. On Thursdays we have Mass here. There are about a dozen priests whom we invite on a rotating basis. Some guys we don't invite back." Eyes twinkle, eyebrows arch. "You can tell the ones who feel uncomfortable. Sometimes it's our simplicity; others are afraid of the poverty or the neighborhood."

Marlys pushes away the empty plate and leans back. "If we didn't pray together the guests would eventually know, even if they don't know we pray. There would be a different air, a sense of loss."

The doorbell pierces the quiet. Marlys admits a faded and worn man with beautiful manners and a gentle Southern voice. He wants food stamp information. He needs to use the telephone.

Her chuckle punctuates her return. She and the visitor have shared a joke. "I was cautious when I came here, shy but not afraid. Iowa gives a basic security. There you don't need to be wary of people, and I've only been really afraid here twice. This place is a whole new ballgame for this country girl from Iowa."

The old brown pickup truck thrums over the gravel and into the back yard. It is 12:30 p.m. and Louis is home for lunch. Today is the weekly appointment with Harvesters, a warehouse supplying low-cost food and household products to soup kitchens and charitable organizations. Once there, Louis swiftly stocks his rolling cart with cartons of canned vegetables, cases of clothes detergent, boxes of dried beans (kidney, lima, frijoles negros). From the pallets he selects what he knows the house will use, avoiding the items which tend to backlog in the basement.

This dark, cool cave of a building formerly sheltered a moving company and the interior dimemsions speak of furniture loads instead of grocery store. Here you take what you can use from what is available. Salted cashews and peanuts are here today; so are granola bars. Next week it might be Twinkies and Fruit Loops. At seven and a half cents a pound it's all a bargain. This bounty will feed the guests and also help to fill 150 grocery sacks for the Saturday giveaway.

At the loading dock the pickup is ready, tailgate down, and Louis's arms snake through his selections, choosing the heavy cartons for the foundation, yogurt and toilet paper on the top.

By 2:00 p.m. all is stashed and Thomas gathers a gallon of paint, a roller and brush and heads for a third-floor bedroom which aches for a fresh coat. Thomas is a Missouri farmer, the drawl of the midlands rolls out of his mouth, soft as butter. He is tall and lanky, built for bluejeans. Five years of Air Force living and a year at Conception Abbey Seminary bring him to summer here. It has been an eye opener. The regimentation of service and school are at odds with the casual chaos of the house.

"At first I thought this place was a mad house. How did they get anything done? But now I see the flow." Thomas carefully removes the gallon lid and, kneeling, begins to stir the paint, a sleepy shade of cream. "This is a lot more than a summer experience. I'll be able to use in future ministry a lot of what I learn here. It's bound to affect me for the rest of my life." Driplessly a slap of cream slides into the roller pan. "The experience speaks of Jesus to me. Patience, endurance, more than food or drink. The people peck away at you. You think you're at your wit's end. Jesus gives me strength to continue. I see Jesus in the staff, in their perseverence. And in the guests. The other day a drunk wino fell and hit his head on the curb. Real fast a lot of other street people were there trying to help. Yeah, God works in them too."

The painting is deliberate, long careful rectangles slip off the roller and onto the wall. Thomas steps back to examine his progress.

"The amount of food is amazing. It shows the over-production of our society. Companies like bakeries make so much, and charge so much, and give so much away, and still make money.

"People enjoy what they get here, not just the food. Look at everyone who hangs around after dinner. It's not just for the food that they come."

It is late afternoon; the clock shows just after 4:00 p.m. when Mary Vincent and Peggy Peterson roll in. They've been coming around for years; their names appear often on the volunteer calander. Their services are required immediately because a crate of peaches needs radical surgery.

"Peaches really go when they're ripe."

"Come on, slimy lettuce is worse than this."

"Remember when we did that bushel of bad radishes? They're the worst."

Mary bubbles, "I keep coming to give back a bit of what I've got. My house is warm and cool appropriately, my husband is great, and my kids aren't on drugs. I like the people here; they don't worry about their BMW's in the parking lot."

Peggy excises bruises, "This place provides balance in my life. It reminds me of my needs and my greeds. I have a real sense of kinship here. See, the people in fancy neighborhoods have the same kinds of inner needs, just that some of them are protected by money."

Mary tries to scratch her nose with the wrist of a juicy hand, "This place is so willing to share their world with us. We're not all willing to accept it."

"A level of honesty here."

"No facades."

"Some volunteers come like 'Lady Bountiful,' but they don't stay."

"This is more spiritual than church. This is the Christian life lived out."

By 4:30 p.m. the rest of the crew gathers in the front hall. A young woman from Habitat for Humanity escorts six teenage girls. Newcomers, nervous, they shift from foot to foot, wanting to giggle, and afraid to, they whisper behind their hands.

Marlys has often introduced first-timers to the geography and sociology of the house kitchen. Her organization and verbal economy are a well-practiced routine. Group divided, work stations established, paring knives produced, chicken presented, vegetables retrieved, staff introduced, timing reviewed.

Secure in the certainty of assigned work, the knot of girls let free a collective inaudible sigh of relief and turn to their tasks.

This kind of volunteering has its rough side. The neighborhood is like a soup at the edge of simmer. The surface is calm but just below the ingredients bump and chaff, waiting to boil. The dining room is often the same. If the night is hot or it has been a long time since the checks came, one man jostling another may trigger anger which escalates to violence before the next heartbeat.

The tables are set by 5:15 p.m., the corn shucked and stacked golden and naked, ready for the pot. Potatoes have been put to boil in institution-huge aluminum pots. The care in preparation reflects the house motto, "We only serve what we ourselves would eat." The afternoon is warm and soft and dappled sun touches the side yard as guests line up for impromptu pre-dinner socialization. The staff drifts in from work. Jane Heavin, a social worker with troubled youngsters, is followed by Dennis Coday who is with the diocesan Catholic newspaper. As they enter, the sounds of the waiting crowd shift slightly into a higher range, then a shout, then a scream. There's a fight. Jane and Dennis are out the front door. The drama is not in the gathered group, but across 31st Street in the parking lot. Crazy Joe is down on the asphalt, unconscious, a steady rapid pool of blood pulsing a ruby halo around his head. His assailant is only slightly less drunk, a bottle grasped in one hand and the offending stick in another.

Jane and Dennis swiftly assess the damage. The paramedics will be needed. Dennis goes for the phone. Wet towels arrive. Joe's eyes flicker. He is helped to a low concrete wall, and Jane applies pressure to the ugly cut beneath his tangled hair. Others, on their way to dinner, slow but do not stop to gape. He's in good hands; they've seen it all before.

Joe, Jane and Dennis go to the hospital. The crowd quiets as the dining room opens. Sister Jan, the "Sergeant," takes her place at the door. It is 6:00 p.m., dinner time.

Guests sit at plastic-covered tables set with Kansas City Royals plastic cups and napkins celebrating Halley's Comet 1986, "a cosmic affair."

Brother Louis asks for someone to offer a prayer. A male voice responds from the back table. The guests rise, reform the line and wind through the kitchen where their plates are filled.

Many are regulars, known by name. For most there is comraderie. For others this meal is a simple necessity; they eat and run.

Delmar James is here tonight, an articulate, quiet Vietnam vet who was a draftsman and mapmaker during the war. He's all right tonight but occasionally goes off the wall.

Tom has come. He eats wholeheartedly and praises the cook for the wonderful chicken. He offers sweeping services for after dinner.

The line shuffles forward. The Habitat girls are now at home, easy with the diners. They do their share of kidding. One guest suggests a date, reducing his intended to a scarlet blush.

Seated in the middle room is a sweet old woman without teeth who details this handicap to every ear. Close by sits an elderly black gentleman wearing a straw boater, who ritualizes the meal. He takes his regular seat and presides over his table, leading the conversation, dispensing advice, like the firm and gentle father of a slightly unruly brood.

By 7:30 p.m. 220 people have been fed. Two of the three dining rooms are empty, wiped and swept. The sun is low and most diners have wandered away. A few linger, a woman in red and white culottes who has been washing plates for an hour rinses out the sink. Louis has handed out bus fares, settled a scratching, hair-pulling fight between two women on the front porch, deflected an aerosol sniffer in the backyard.

Sister Jan leans against the door frame. Tiredness shows around her eyes and in her slight frame. She works full time as a lawyer at Legal Aid and comes home to police the dining room. The smallest of all the staff members at five feet, she nonetheless is full of authority and even the biggest, drunkest visitors yield to her.

"The attraction of this place is the guests, their stories, their lives, their ability to know whether you are real.

There are parts of me that aren't whole, and when the guests challenge me or accuse me, then I need to take that challenge and figure out if what they say is true. One man came in disruptive, angry. He was abusive, so I asked him to take his plate out and eat on the porch. He yelled at me, 'It's because I'm gay, isn't it? It's because I'm gay.' Then I need to think, is this a discrimination I harbor? Was that any part of my thinking?

"This house, these people really refuel my values; the experience constantly reminds me of God's gift of miracles. We *do* have multiplication of loaves and fishes. Our first Easter we were expecting 40 guests for dinner. A young man showed up with the vegetable 20 minutes before we were going to serve. He had one crockpot of carrots. There was plenty for everyone. Over and over again, when we need something, we don't even have to voice that need outside the house and we receive it. I think the miracle we like best is when guests who are angry can reconcile themselves. There is a gift of peace here in our dining rooms. People have to live in our very violent society, and they can come here and let themselves be at peace."

Jan peers wistfully from behind dark-rimmed glasses. "The longer I'm here the more I wonder at the mystery of how do people survive this life of poverty and lack of safety and do it with good humor. I've come to the conclusion that it is a total faith which comes from being stripped of everything."

As the dining room door is about to be latched for the night, a weary little band of travellers arrives. It is Marie hauling her children. Marie has zombie eyes. Life has gotten to be more than she can handle. She dumps 6-week-old Brittany into the eager embrace of Marlys and releases 18-month-

old Matthew to Jane. They come often. The house is an oasis at which to shed burdens.

Matthew is fed by Jane who has a circus of noises to accompany the loaded spoon. Matthew giggles. He is the staff darling and gets his ration of loving in their arms.

Brittany's clothes are soaked. Has she been changed all day? In clean sleepers she is held and baby-talked. Food for the body and the tender spirit too.

The community speaks with affection about the guests and the dinner just completed. For them, the meal is where it all happens.

"The meal is the time when I've felt closest to God," Dennis shares. "Although we had decided, as a community, to give each staff member a night off from supper, no one has taken advantage of this opportunity. Everyone wants to be at supper because if you miss that, you've missed everything. It is here that we recognize Jesus in the breaking of the bread."

Nettie listens and responds, "When I came here, I didn't know what to expect. I was scared to death. I've learned more here than in two years of college. Dinner is a high for me, a real source of energy. I get so much from the guests. Dinner time is totally consuming; it's all you are. Sometimes I wonder, Why can't we do more? Are we doing more harm than good by simply recycling people? But each night when I go in there, I know we're doing something right."

For Marlys it is the same. "For me, the least favorite way of describing ourselves is as a 'soup kitchen.' The guests are invited into our home. We are as we are; they come as they are; and we share."

It is getting late and this is community prayer night. The group gathers for scripture and popcorn from Marlys' family farm. Into the quiet flow the words of Isaiah.

This, rather, is the fasting that I wish;
releasing those bound unjustly,
untying the thongs of the yoke;
Setting free the oppressed,
breaking every yoke;
Sharing your bread with the hungry,
sheltering the oppressed and the homeless;
Clothing the naked when you see them,
and not turning your back on your own.
Then your light shall break forth like the
dawn,
and your wound shall quickly be healed;
Your vindication shall go before you,
and the glory of the Lord shall be your rear
guard (Is. 58:6-8).

The lights are dimmed and slides taken over the seasons in the dining rooms flash across the wall. Like all families, this family freezes moments on film at holiday times, and caught in the glare of the flash are faces eagerly turned toward the camera, surrounded by accordian paper turkeys, adorned in Halloween costumes, displaying the hats and scarves given at Christmas.

Voices speak quietly in the darkness:

"Look how good Tom looks in that picture!"

"That's Joe by the turkey; he's been dead a year now."

A slide of Frank rolls onto the screen. There he is, proud with his shopping cart, his collection basket. There is a pause. Frank has not always delighted the house with his boisterous and combative behavior. Many a meal he has taken on the front porch in isolation from others. Now they comment on his ill health and wonder at his continued ability to hang onto life.

It is at moments of reflection like these that the hovering presence of Sister Joan Kane is tangible. Joan died in an automobile accident in July 1986. She still lives daily in the joys, sorrows, aches and pleasures of every corner of this dwelling. On staff since 1981, Joan shared her deep joy, inner freedom and good humor constantly. Being home full-time, she lived the ministry of availability to the guests: listening with interest, opening herself easily to each person at the door, each caller on the phone. Hers was not a somber, fretful caring. Funny things seemed to happen to her more often than to others, and as "the best storyteller ever" she shared in laughter. Joan had her likes and dislikes, one of the latter being summer heat, another being early morning. But nothing seemed too much for this bundle of energy. "It can be done, regardless" was a motto for her. When Joan Kane died, the "REGARDLESS" sweatshirt, so lovingly given as a birthday gift by the community, was buried with her.

Her legacy of joy still breathes in this house. It was Frank who gave testimony to this goodness at the time of her funeral when he said, "I'd a been here if I had to crawl."

Now darkness embraces the house, the street lights star-prick the night. The urban noises have gentled, punctuated only occasionally by the scream of sirens. The many scattered moments of the day are knitted together and given whole to those gathered here as Louis reads the words of Dorothy Day.

The most significant thing about the Catholic Worker is poverty, some say.

The most significant thing is community, others say.

We are not alone anymore.

But the final word is love. At times it has been, in the words of Father Zossima, a harsh and dreadful thing, and our very faith in love has been tried by fire. We cannot love God unless we love each other, and to love we must know each other. We know God in the breaking of bread, and we know each other in the breaking of bread, and we are not alone anymore. Heaven is a banquet and life is a banquet, too, even with a crust, where there is companionship.

We have all known the long loneliness and we have learned that the only solution is love and that love comes with community (*The Long Loneliness,* p. 276).

Obonaudsawin Farm

Lexington, Michigan

If you stand on the gravelled driveway which leads to the side door of the Obonaudsawin farmhouse, with your back toward the dwelling, you look out over the garden, a two-acre delight. Now in high summer, the mounded-up rows of well-mulched vegetables blossom, thrive and produce in a way that would make Peter Maurin's country heart burst with pleasure. It does the same for Pat Oliss. This surprises her because she is a woman of varied background to whom farming is not first nature.

Obonaudsawin farm, all 99 acres of thriving fertility, is a direct outgrowth of the marriage of the Catholic Worker's call to return to the land with Pat's drive, intelligence and curiosity about all things natural.

Pat is a city child, raised in an orphanage, with years in a religious order doing work that was more cerebral than physical. She says, "A friend became involved with Day House (a Catholic worker house in center-city Detroit). She told me about it. But I *knew* if I went there I'd get hooked. They finally got me. I started going every Sunday. At this time my life was divided, and what really attracted me was that the people at the house shared a common faith in the gospels. They were very into serving people, very into living in community. The personal risks they were taking and the lifestyle they were living were very familiar to me. I got really drawn into it."

Pat, at 45, is a small, comely woman, solid and capable, with a head of enviable silver curls. A laugh which would be logical in a six-footer rolls out of her. Genuinely a woman of authority and passionate conviction, a doer and a dreamer, she is the bailing wire that holds this farm together. "There is real need in me to live the way I believe. The only thing that made sense to me was living off the land, meeting my own needs, not oppressing anyone. I'd never seen a farm, never grown a garden."

In her belief, and steeped in the writings of Peter Maurin, she looked for others to share the dream. Though some told Pat she didn't know what she was getting into, she wrote an article for the October 20, 1978, issue of *On The Edge*, the newspaper of Day House.

The Catholic Worker Movement is alive in Detroit—alive, vibrant, growing! Yes, but missing an essential component: the farm. So, dare we dream again! Dare we risk again! Let's start a farm!

Why a farm?

1. Farming is an alternate way of life. A way of life that can be minimally associated with the multi-nations and their oppressive course. Farming can enable us to be less caught up in the materialism of our age. Also it naturally lends itself to communal living and sharing and can bring us into harmony with God's earth.

2. A farm can offer a healthy setting for those unwanted in our cities. It can offer work with dignity.

4. It might even be able to become the beginnings of some communal type farm community.

5. We can learn much at a farm: new skills, productive labor, cooperative sharing, respect for God's nature and a host of virtues from patience to perseverance and who knows what hidden assets lie waiting our venture!

And so was born a miracle, not overnight, not in ease, but a miracle forged in struggle, a miracle of persistance and prayer, a miracle of faith.

Pat's printed invitation was answered by a family with four children and an 18-year-old young woman. They began to meet regularly and to talk of Peter Maurin's dream. In a short time they were searching for land. With money from Pat's community and from the family, they were able to make a downpayment in October 1979. Babes in the woods, total neophytes they were.

Pat recalls, "A miracle was the prior farmer. He came three days a week. He taught us how to farm, plowed our fields for the first oat crop. He left us his chickens and feed for them. He called and came often. He taught us everything."

Through the years the community has been blessed with temporary volunteers who have brought farming skills with them. One of the first was Joe Crowley, a gentle-eyed man whose face is partially obscured by an enormous black beard. During college he had begun to explore the ties between Christianity and pacifism and concluded that his call was to a self-sufficient simple life.

Joe smiles, "I had a dream of living on a farm like this without knowing Catholic Worker farms existed. When I read about this farm I knew this was it and came planning to stay forever."

But Joe recognized during that first year a difficulty which plagues the farm to this day—the struggle of community building. He, like many, came with a Utopian vision of the farm. He thought that the inhabitants, fired by the gospels and the teachings of Maurin and Day, would quickly become an intimate community with bonds strengthened by prayer, study, common goals and hard work. He expected a lofty crew and found "ordinary people just like anywhere else." Disillusionment and loneliness caused him to leave after seven months. But he couldn't stay away. He returned two years later with his bride, the bubbling and beautiful Rose. She, a life-long city girl, looks as if she were born to farming. Freshfaced, long-haired and freckled, she exudes what might be called "that country look" reminiscent of movies like "State Fair."

Sitting in a well-used easy chair in the living room, Rose scrapes baby carrots, thinnings from the garden patch, which will be a part of dinner. She remembers, "I came because of Joe and because the values of the Catholic Worker were already a part of me, especially working with the poor." Though she believes in the work, she found the farm a hard place in which to find her niche. Sent to weed in the garden, she would become discouraged at not being able to tell the weeds from the plants. The people around her spoke knowingly about the benefits of rye versus oats or the value of green manure. She was lost. Gradually through introspection and experience she has become more self-assured and has found her special role.

"The benefit of me here is that I'm a good community builder. I see the dramatic necessity of people who are willing to work through problems in community, and I'm good at seeing what problems are there. Because of this I'm willing to confront unpleasant situations, much more than Joe."

Joe favors long periods of solitude, but Rose sees the need to weave themselves into the lives of others. "We live in intense community." That intensity is increased by physical proximity since the community is housed under one small roof, except for Pat who inhabits a beautiful, fuctional, self-constructed wigwam several hundred yards away.

Monday mornings are reserved for spiritual meeting which the residents take turns in planning. They try to bring where they are spiritually to these sessions. In addition, the group attempts to reserve Wednesday mornings for the reading of the Holy Office and for scripture. They worship together at the local parish where Rose leads the singing and provides music with her guitar.

Tuesday nights are kept aside for the community's business. On this night all things relating to the farm and its workers are open for discussion. What crops shall we plant next year? What can be done organically to rid the tomatoes of cutworms? The potatoes are developing blight again. How much hospitality can we manage? How many volunteers can we count on for next year?

Some issues are resolved quickly; long-term ones are voted on solely by the members of the group who have made a serious commitment to remain for an extended period. This decision-making process was a result of hard learning after short-termers voted to plant crops they would not stay to harvest.

One of Joe and Rose's greatest contributions to the community is an exquisite red-haired 7-month-old, Theresa Rose. She was born at home with everyone in encouraging attendance, in deepest winter, an almost Christmas presence. Though she is unaware of her significance, she has become everyone's child, going willingly to each, smiling for all, bonding them together. Prior to her arrival Joe began work on a several room extension of the farmhouse to shelter the three of them and to free more room for hospitality.

If Joe the intensely committed worker, Rose the community builder, and Theresa their child have come to function as the heart of Obonaudsawin, the wisdom figure is Hazan Ordway, a white-haired, full-bearded patriarch well into his 70's. He has known the Catholic Worker since its seminal years and has the credentials of being a loving and believing student at the round table of Peter Maurin. Though he is not yet a permanent member of the farm, he has had several long sojourns there and is now in a discernment about remaining forever.

"I was in the Marists for two years. I thought I wanted to be a priest and went on the to the Trappists at Gethsemani. But the Catholic Worker was my calling and the religious life prepared me for it. I had heard Dorothy lecture at Catholic U. Her zeal for justice for the worker, her desire to correct the injustice in the working world was tremendous."

Fired by her message, he met Peter who "called me to farming communities where

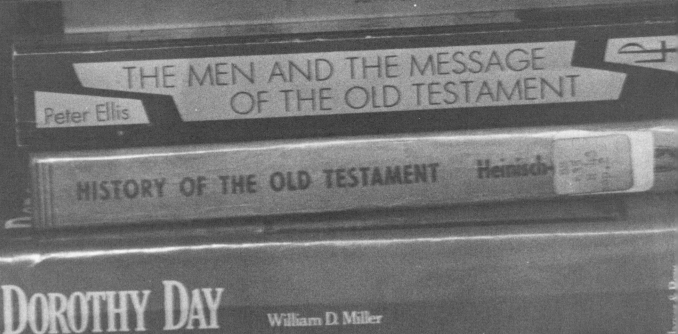

THE MEN AND THE MESSAGE
OF THE OLD TESTAMENT

Peter Ellis

HISTORY OF THE OLD TESTAMENT   Heinisch

DOROTHY DAY
A BIOGRAPHY   William D. Miller

Poverty in American Democracy

MICHIGAN FOUR SEASONS   HAIKU POETRY   Robert Rentschler

EXPLAINING THE GOSPEL

THE D ASPARAGUS

The Ministry of HEALING   White

there is learning like the monastic communities of Europe." He continues, "The whole movement is a miracle, the very way it has grown. It is God's work. People have been inspired by the Holy Spirit, their hearts being moved to continue."

Hazan is a veteran of many Catholic Worker houses and farms, including the original community at Easton, Pennsylvania, and the Tivoli farm on Staten Island. A long marriage to a wife who felt no call to the Catholic Worker did nothing to dampen his zest for the values and vision. Now, the marriage annulled, he hopes to work the land and share the wisdom for the rest of his days.

Guided by the wisdom of Dorothy and Peter and fueled by faith and perseverance, the farm has come a long way toward the dream which Pat spelled out in her article. The choice of a life of voluntary poverty has freed the group from much of the slavery of materialism. The farmhouse, while comfortable, is extremely simple and the furniture is obviously a collection of gifts and scavenging, not chosen for style. Clothing is more for comfort than beauty. For all this they are rich, since they have few wants and lack nothing essential.

The farm chores are managed with second-hand equipment and the wheat cut with a horse-drawn combine. Everything is saved; everything used. Nothing is discarded. The effect is not one of parsimony but of enormous care. To view vegetable parings as chicken feed or compost material is to honor them, to recognize that even what is garbage to others has a role here in nurturing life again.

There has been a determined move toward self-sufficiency, heating the house with wood harvested from the forest, grinding their wheat for flour, eating deliciously vegetarian because they have no money for meat and they seldom slaughter. They even capture their own bee swarms.

"I was out in the garden and I saw Joe dash out of the asparagus patch," Pat recalls. "He ran into the house and back out again banging pot lids together. A swarm of honeybees had landed, and Joe knew that banging lids together quieted them. We brought up a hive and they went in."

Pat figures they are 80 percent self-sufficient, buying only oil, some spices, salt, rice and sugar. Even their wine comes from wild grapes which have taken root. Her next dream is wind-powered electricity to make them less dependent on public utilities.

In the midst of this independence they have been able to share their abundance, first with Day House, then with a soup kitchen run by a small Baptist congregation in Port Huron.

In order to preserve the bounty for year-round use, Rose, Joe, Hazan and other volunteers spend many hours canning and freezing hundreds and hundreds of pounds of vegetables and fruits. Root crops, cabbages, pumpkins and winter squash are stored in the cellar for the short, cold days of January.

People in struggle or in need of retreat from the pressure of urban society come to Obonaudsawin Farm. Some guests come regularly to be nurtured by this gentle group. Some come, are refreshed and depart never to reappear. Some are too damaged to participate in the work of the farm; others are delighted to be included in healthy helpful labor. One wonderful summer the farm sheltered 13 guests and workers.

However, the formation of a respectably sized permanent family continues to elude them. Pat's dream is for about 15 adults, married or single, to make a firm commitment. "Beyond that we lose intimacy."

In distress about the problem, Pat put the farm in a caretaker's hands for a year and travelled around the country from house to house on the Catholic Worker network.

"I didn't know how to build community. Was I doing something wrong? Do I intimidate people?"

The year of prayer and thought led her back to Michigan. "When I came back after the trip I was alone for a month. It was so hard. A lot of deterioration had taken place while I was gone. The house was filled with mice. I was so discouraged. There was so much work, and I had $11 to last me a month. One day two women from the parish came and volunteered help, then two men from a charismatic prayer group came and fixed the pump on the well. I needed chicken feed and had no money, so I called a local farmer and asked for corn and oats. He not only brought them, he got us $200 credit at the mill."

It was at that time that Joe and Rose arrived, and so did some donations. Pat began to see a glimmer of growth and today is hopeful that God will provide all those who are needed to do the work.

A young family is now considering building on the land and making the choice for the community. Joe has also been aware of their influence on the neighbors. "It's a witness to the people of the area, to their middle-classness. We've chosen to live a radically different life. They see there is another way of being, living."

The farm has been a hard taskmaster, demanding the acquisition of many skills, stretching all toward greater competence. Joe comments, "Sometimes it has been incredibly hard." On the living-room shelves *Easy Essays* by Peter Maurin sits next to volumes on animal husbandry and canning procedures. *The Long Loneliness* by Dorothy Day is wedged between organic gardening publications.

Everyone is preoccupied with restoring the land instead of treating it only as a production site. Certain fields which were heavily treated with chemicals have been lovingly coaxed back to their natural states. The reverence for God's gift of land has been formalized in a written statement.

Obonaudsawin... It is the Algonquin word for life.

Strange, perhaps strange as the Indian way is always strange to Western thinking.

Strange, perhaps strange as the words of Chief Seattle in 1854 when he gave these words to Washington when the white man asked to buy "their" land.

"How can you buy or sell the sky, the warmth of the land. The idea is strange to us. We do not own the freshness of the air and the sparkle of the water, how can you buy them?... The land is sacred to us."

And so Obonaudsawin is strange to us
And into its rhythm we wish to enter.
For in the Indian way of thinking
Land is central to life
Life was created from it
Life was sustained by it
And in death life returns to the land to begin the life process anew....

We wish to learn

Not how to own, control, possess, determine

But rather how to be in rhythm with the life cycles about us.

Stand and gaze at Obonaudsawin Farm. Absorb the visual feast. See the crops lovingly nurtured, the sheep grazing easily, the ripple of wind-touched grain, golden and ready. Witness the cow, Lady Frances, waiting to be milked and the tomatoes, green but full of promise of food for those in need. Hear the easy interchange of guests from the city. The land seems happy, not unnaturally forced but sharing its bounty willingly. Feel the spirits of Peter Maurin and Dorothy Day. You can almost see them smile, and know their work lives on.

Noonday Farm

Winchendon Springs, Massachusetts

If you are searching for a community fashioned around prayer, labor and laughter, with a healthy seasoning of music to sweeten your noons and nights, you may find yourself standing at the end of a rural lane in Massachusetts. On your right, among the ferns, will be a substantial sign proclaiming WINCHENDON SPRINGS: WORKING TOGETHER. You have arrived at Noonday Farm Catholic Worker House, a community of individuals, tested, faith-filled and free, working together. In the kitchen, on the porch, or perhaps in the garden you will find

Bill Beardslee and his wife, Lisa Mahar, Louise Cochran and her husband, Jim Levinson, Michael Harank, Eveline MacDougall and Robert Hurwitz. Their journeys to this house have probably been more complicated than yours.

Jim Levinson, a curly haired and bearded Jew, possessor of a Ph.D. in Agricultural Economics and International Nutrition, is seated at the piano.

"I spent years with the Foreign Aid Department of the State Department; a half-dozen years in India; and two in Bangladesh. But I developed some serious questions about the nature of United States involvement in Asia and Latin America. Every United States program in Bangladesh was widening the gap between the haves and the have-nots. I was craving something more direct; I wanted to do something with the people I was writing about."

He and Louise returned from the East searching for something more: community, ministry, simplicity, resistance, but having no idea how to make that possible.

"In 1981 Noah (their son) was born, and we began to ask ourselves, What does it mean to have a child? We had friends who, when children came, withdrew from social justice activities and involved themselves in the material betterment of the child."

Jim crosses his ankles, feet naked in sandals, and stretches to remember. "We took a working trip around the world. In Israel we saw a working kibbutz, our first experience of intentional community. Louise and I were so drawn. Then in the Philippines I did some work for the Marcos government. I knew for sure that I was on the wrong side. But while I was there I walked into a used-book store. There was a 1971 Holy Cross Quarterly on the Berrigan brothers. We devoured it."

The thirst was quenched in that moment. "We had to ask the questions of how long we could go on compromising." Returning to Boston they discovered the Catholic Worker at Haley House, an urban soup kitchen.

In the company of Haley House members Jim celebrated the Feast of the Holy Innocents in protest before the pillars of the Pentagon. "It was conversion, a moment of spiritual intensity. Blood and ashes. For me nothing would ever be the same again."

Jim and Louise gave up a 14 room house filled with the treasures of the world and moved into Haley House.

"I read lots of Dorothy Day. I really responded to that New York radical journalist of the '30s who fought battles and came to a deeper spiritual understanding. But I also responded to the earthy French peasant Peter Maurin."

Jim flashes his 1000-watt grin. "I finally decided I didn't want to read about farming; I wanted to get out there and do it."

In the two years in Boston "we began to visualize a community which would be better adapted to families than an urban soup

kitchen." Winchendon Springs, the classic Catholic Worker antidote to the miseries of the city, was the answer.

Jim's wife, Louise Cochran, is a striking woman with her intense pale eyes sheltered beneath well-arched brows, elegant fingers and economical body gracefully borne. Her spiritual journeying, "the most important part of my life," has been a global experience, from her childhood as the daughter of a Presbyterian minister through the lecture halls of Harvard Divinity, from the kibbutz in Israel to the poverty of Bangladesh.

"I felt called to serve. I went to a Tibetan monastery for six weeks for a meditation course. My days were very ordered. I fasted; we kept silence. I was scared. I was going as a seeker. Would Jim still love me when this was over?" A wash of re-imagined pain flows over her face—and excitement. "I knew my life would be different. I received authentic spiritual teaching. I could assent to everything I was taught. By chance it was during Lent." The confluence of the Buddhist and Christain experiences makes her eyes twinkle.

Back in Boston, almost on the eve of ministerial ordination, she changed her mind. "I realized how much the ministry was like the corporate world. That was just what Jim and I were trying to escape from."

At the Easter Vigil celebrated at Haley House in 1983 Louise professed her faith and became a Catholic. Her hands dart out and inscribe a wide circle in the air. "I was led to the Catholic Worker through this wonderful succession of experiences."

But Haley House was hard, living in one room, a baby to mother. "There were crazy hours, and Noah didn't have a regular bedtime. I was afraid of violence and hid out with Noah (often at the apartment of Henri Nouwen who made it available for respite), and worked the elderly shift. The house was crazy: the phone, the doorbell, the arguments about hospitality. I wanted to leave. I had lost a lot of my outside support system. The Alanthus work (a sustained vigil at AVCO Systems Division, a major MX-missile contractor) was energizing, reflecting on it."

Then, as if by miracle, Haley House acquired sufficient money to buy a farm.

Lisa Mahar sits at the communal table, the sunlight which floods the bay window behind her dappling her hair. Surrounded by stacks of mail, she invests the morning in responding to the gifts and inquiries of supporters. Her handwriting is beautiful, round and flowing, a sign of many hours bent over copybooks.

"We began to look for this place in the fall of 1983, and this was one of the first we saw. It was in terrible shape. The kitchen was gutted; there were rotten sills; there was a disabled truck in the yard. We looked at other places, but with 18 acres and 13 rooms this one had the best possibilities. It's on a dead-end road, so it is a great place for kids.

We finally realized that the need for work allowed us to put our own stamp on the place."

Lisa is merry; she sees humor everywhere and seems to be always on the edge of laughter. "Being in on the beginnings," her eyes roll in memory of the mess, "allowed us to create everything from scratch."

Her husband, Bill Beardslee, is painting walls in an addition built to make more hospitality possible. When he's not rolling paint or pulling weeds or harvesting produce, he is a United Church of Christ minister. Now he wears overalls and a sweatband. His wire-rimmed glasses gleam.

Bill spent a long time not really sure of what his life should come to. Two major decisions came together as the divining rod which led him here. First was the commitment to enter Andover-Newton Seminary where between class assignments he sandwiched in volumes on the nature and reality of community living. Second was the choice to join in the Alanthus community in Medford, Massachusetts, where he and others focused on the vigil at AVCO Systems Division. During this three-year encampment, nagging questions persisted: "How do Lisa and I sustain for the long haul the changes we have made? How do we raise a family? How do we move toward a more simple lifestyle? do the works of mercy? keep a balance?"

Bill and Lisa connected with Haley House through the peace movement, and met Jim and Louise. "I was impressed with the peace and justice stuff of the Catholic Worker," Bill says, "but I didn't like the city. The thought of doing this in a rural setting was really exciting."

The dream of horticulture, an early one, began to bear fruit. "I read Peter Maurin, and he articulated things about the land and the integrity of work which are really exciting to me."

Michael Harank is perched on a broken-down couch on the porch. He is a dark, intense man. His whole body, not just mouth and mind, enter into conversation. Serious, he is often the first to see the philosophical ramifications of a comment, the broad application of a voiced opinion. He is adept at sending the verbal flow far afield and gathering in the ripples to bring it safely home.

Michael grew up in a working class French Canadian family in Lynn, Massachusetts. He recalls a painful childhood, capped by the experience of his much-loved older brother's imprisonment for draft resistance. Attracted by the gentle personalism of Dorothy Day, he arrived at the Catholic Worker in New York City in October 1977.

Four years there convinced him that all the work and all the need of the city streets which poured in through the door of Mary House were not enough to cauterize his own wounds. "I decided I needed time to be quiet and face some issues. So I went to New Mexico, to a Benedictine Monastery. I spent six months coming to grips with the cross of my own life, coming toward the Resurrection."

Leaning forward, he speaks intensely. "I want life, and life more abundantly. *I survived a lot of years; now I want to live.*"

On his face is a smile of acceptance. "You have to face your own darkness. There is nowhere to run."

Moving from the "borderline institution" of Mary House to the smaller community of Haley House, Michael eventually discerned the desire to become a registered nurse. When the farm became a possibility, he committed to living there for the duration of his studies. A social being, Michael knew he needed this group to sustain him through the loneliness of school. "Community is when we become fully conscious of our wounds, our vulnerability, our neediness, our poverty. Community is what happens when God breaks through!"

The dreams of all became flesh when the closing papers were signed on May 1, 1984, the anniversary of the Catholic Worker Movement. Purchased were field and stream, including the forest home of blue heron, and a rambling gray-blue house dating from 1789.

The determination of the little group was immediately tested by the horns-down charge of a wild "attack goat" which claimed this property as his own. Michael wrestled the beast to submission and locked him in a shed, henceforth and forever to be known as the goat room. The real work was just beginning.

In the words of Isaiah, (58:6,7):

"The kind of fasting I want is this: Remove the chains of oppression and the yoke of injustice, and let the oppressed go free. Share your food with the hungry and open your homes to the homeless poor. Give clothes to those who have nothing to wear, and do not refuse to help your own relatives. Then my favor will shine on you like the morning sun... .

The initial group, including Eileen Lawter of Mary house, was determined to give lift to that word of the Lork in a living community, Noonday Farm.

The property was in near ruin. Marijuana plants grew in abundance, paint peeled, windows were broken. The group, which for a short time included Eileen Lawter of Mary House, was forced to take refuge on the second floor while mending the damage, planting the gardens and providing hospitality. Lisa voices the vivid determination in those hostile beginnings: "The Catholic Worker farm has great possibilities for families that we wanted to enflesh."

Always, amid shovel and brush, the focus was on building community, a unity with one another in prayer, resistance and love.

Michael says, "We made the decision to spend the first year together, learning each other, focusing on developing our own sense of community. We must function in a communal way. Now we can."

"Unless a faith-focused community is in place, the work fails," Lisa observes. "It looks like navel-gazing to some, and we have taken a lot of flak for it. But the quality of community life and work are interdependent. There's no way to form community without a faith focus."

This is hard, hard work, especially in a society which often seems genuinely dedicated to mangling relationships, where ego rather than other is the basis for judgment. "There are no secrets about people's idiosyncracies after three years," Lisa comments. "We have had a lot of challenging situations which we have had to work out one by one." The long-term commitment to the farm and the relationships allows us to work out our differences; every challenge doesn't throw the whole thing into question."

Jim grins, "For me this is a place where we could make community, grow food for the soup kitchen, do hospitality for the elderly and the poor, do some retreat work, and try and follow the example of Peter Maurin and the Catholic Worker farm. I'd be out at 5:30 a.m. working. I'd get exasperated, martyred, where were the others? I was much more into 'do' than 'be.' We had a blowup. It could have been the end of the community. There was a lot of hurt and it took months but we hung in there.

"My biggest struggle is accepting the end of the day, the week, when there is still so much undone."

There is no anxiety in his frame, no tension, as he observes, "I'm comfortable with where we are. It has been tougher going than I expected. I need to be careful in a personal-interpersonal sense. I work on relaxing a bit."

To make all this togetherness possible, the house provides large, airy, welcoming rooms. The main gathering place is an enormous space dominated by the grand piano, a wood-burning stove, a dining table and a big sitting area with springless couches and frayed chairs. Picture windows display the valley beyond.

Winter and summer, the day begins at 7:30 a.m. Adults and children wander down from the private family quarters. Yawns, coffee cups and cereal bowls dominate the first moments of assembly. This is a gentle time, a time to portion out the responsibility of the day.

Childcare revolves among the adults in the summer, but falls to Lisa in the winter as part of the nursery school she runs. Everyone, except Michael the student, is employed to provide for the daily sustenance of the house. Louise works pastorally in a nursing home. Jim is cantor in a synagogue in Athol. He has also taught grade school and high school here in the past. Bill has his own congregation. Everyone shares farm work. Children snuggle against the chill of the morning in their parent's laps as an adult reads an excerpt from a chosen work, perhaps *The Year of Living Dangerously* or Annie Dillard's *Pilgrim at Tinker's Creek*.

Jim sounds a piano, and the community rises to sing. This morning they sing "The Magnificat" in Latin. Song—joyful, robust, melancholy, full of soul—is a hallmark of

Noonday Farm. Selections range from the music of the Brothers of Taize to songs ripe in yearning from the South African Freedom Movement. Classical piano music, Jim's love and others' enjoyment, enriches the day. Here song is the essence of things, song of prayer, song with meals, song with hospitality. Their penchant for the musical has been noted in print.

Jane Alexander, director of the Women's Lunch Place, a Boston soup kitchen, brings several women here for a few days each summer. "They make us feel so comfortable," she said. "They do a cookout, there's swimming and singing around the piano" (New York Times, June 23, 1987).

Jim shared his skills patiently each morning with his 6-year-old son, Noah. First thing after breakfast violin and piano are coaxed to life under Jim's direction and Noah's willing fingers.

Music finds a home here where the hustling life of the city gives way to the creative energy at work in nature. The rhythm of community life and the rhythm of the earth blend to make a harmony which refreshes, heals and reveals the Divine Presence. As Annie Dillard wrote:

> I had been my whole life a bell
> and never knew it
> until at that moment
> I was lifted and struck
> (*Pilgrim at Tinker's Creek*).

Lunch at 1:00 p.m. is lively, commencing with a Quaker hand- holding song:

> Thank you for this food, this food,
> this glorious, glorious food.
> And the animals, and the vegetables
> and the minerals that make it possible.

Bowls of tuna, carrots and celery, pasta salad, plates of bread and cheese circle the table. Hard-working people, they fill their plates. Questions about afternoon swimming from Lisa and Bill's 10-year-old Amber share the air with Bill's comments about the progress of his paint job in the new addition. A recent graduate of the New England Conservatory of Music is a guest. Some thoughts about classical piano duets are aired. Luke, golden and sturdy at 5, shares his morning activities at summer camp.

When the plates are cleared, a chapter from Madeline L'Engle's *A Wrinkle in Time* is read. The last page turned, the children depart except for 2-year-old Dora, who searches out first her mother's lap, then proceeds around the table giving other adults equal time.

The talk drifts to community spirituality. Another round of iced tea is poured into assorted containers, jelly glass to mug.

Lisa is ruminative, going back again over familiar turf. "I struggle with prayer. there is a shifting image of God for me in the male/female aspect. I need to get a daily focus. I struggle and it's hard. I grew up Catholic and would never choose it on my own, but I keep coming back to it. The sacraments, the mystery continue to call and challenge me."

"I was not raised in a particularly religious way, but my family did celebrate the High Holidays and I was bar mitzvahed," says Jim. He has done a lot of thinking about what goes into praying with this house full of Christians. "I consider Jesus as one of my rabbis. As a Jew I can go a long way toward following his life and teaching. I do not find myself comfortable, though, with naming Christ or Yahweh. It isn't a part of my tradition. The same is true about using Jesus' name in common prayer.

"The authenticity of Jesus has been a guide for me for many years," Bill adds. "I can't always be authentic, but I always try." He tips back on his chair. "It's a painful way to be in the world, but it is strengthening, too. This place helps me be my best self in a way other places don't. You can't get away with a lot in community, and I pray that people will accept me for what I am." Bill is a man of significant size, and his gentleness is surprising. "I'm awed by the gift of life. Walking, living in the upside-down world of faith, taking the risk, making the choice of giving in to God. The more we realize here our incapability of doing it alone the more we can do." He laughs, "Why, the fact that 11 people can survive on $29,000 is a *miracle!* I feel rich. I would invite the world to leap, but make sure to do it with community."

Michael's experience blends with Bill's and he leans forward, elbows on the table's edge. "The miracle of humanity in community can't be taken for granted. If a community has no faith, it is only a battleground of egos. Community means sharing a deep sense of vulnerability. That's where grace comes in, when we are wounded, we recognize our poverty, we get the grace to make our wounds visible, to trust."

Eveline MacDougall and Robert Hurwitz arrive from a three-day trip to her family in Minnesota. Eveline is 23 and has a year-long commitment to the community, now almost expired. Robert is somewhat older, stringy, bearded, with a red bandanna tied hat-like around his long hair. He is not a full member of the group; rather, he arrived looking for shelter while working as a carpenter in the area. Nonetheless, he is deeply enmeshed in the life of the farm and has been the major mover and shaker in getting the goat room converted into two hospitality bedrooms.

Eveline has, like many others, come from pain, family and job. She has been healing for a year. She is young and curly haired; the children love her attention. "I left the Catholic church in the sense of attending. I had some disagreements with the men in Rome. Now I have the revelation that I can disagree and still be spiritual. I'm getting well here, by nurturing and being nurtured." This has been a moment for her to get in touch with herself and with the earth.

Dora becomes audibly tired and goes off to bed after a round a liquid kisses. The table cleared, the dishes dispatched, it is community meeting time. After prayer, the issues, already listed, come flowing forth: the creosote smell from the living-room stove, where to keep the compost can, the clothesline problem. This concern has a history. Air ver-

sus sun drying is considered. Placing it over the old septic system is discussed. "Will you sink as you hang?" Lots of laughter. Amber wants a pet mouse. Is this a family or community decision? Ann, a past guest, wishes to return. Will she be welcome? Will she be long-term?

Robert reminds the rest of the precarious transportation situation. Their cars toil on the edge of collapse. He has discovered a real find on the way home from Minnesota, a small pickup truck owned by a bee-keeper, now deceased. The price is perfect. The room for hauling vegetables to Boston is ideal. The community listens carefully. Robert has thoroughly examined the vehicle. They are interested. Who would like to accompany Robert to re-examine it? People volunteer for that and other tasks. As Lisa says, "I'm better at being asked than being mad."

The afternoon grows long; children are tired. They have been in to sit, out to play and back again. Now they want parental attention. The meeting winds down. It has been like all good meetings, some things accomplished, some deferred, some agreed upon, some questions raised. They have learned well how to listen, and how to portion out time and energy.

The children, unwitting instigators of this community, are a treasure. They display none of the runny-nosed, wild-haired, unkempt appearance of the offspring of the hippie communes of the '60s. Five year old Luke sports a fashionable golden rattail. Amber, dark-skinned and warm-natured, is the sought-after playmate of all the others. Noah is quiet, a balance to Luke's flow of words. They match in age and companionship. This farm is a wonderful, wild, safe place to run loose in the business of growing up. At 2, Dora wears "jelly" shoes, and is everyone's child. The only one born on the farm, she has a special sense of place. As an integral part of the group the children help to determine its rhythms—three square meals a day, home in the evenings, time for swing and slide. They mercifully undermine the tendency to super-seriousness and aim the adults' attention toward hospitality for families. Dora is especially talented at provoking laughter with her light-hearted "happy to be on the planet" philosophy.

Michael, though single, is supportive of the family focus. He says it has helped him to deal with some of the pain of his own growing up. He sees this as a specific ministry of the community. "We've taken in women, pregnant and with children. How can this community, made up of families, offer hospitality? One has to think carefully about what hospitality means. It's more than numbers. Emphasis is not on quantity, but on gentle personalism." The group offers others the same hospitality which they offer to the children who are already part of this community.

The fervor and thoughtfulness invested in sheltering has led to political activities against apartheid in South Africa, United States involvement in Nicaragua and the arms race. It has produced vegetables in the garden, enough to serve seven soup kitchens and shelters in Boston.

Bill sees the very existence of Noonday Farm as ministry. "One of the things we're about, the very fact of moving to the land, changing our environment, changing our relationships with each other, is in itself ministry. For there to be systemic structural change in this society, we have to live it."

Louise acknowledges this. "For me, this community is like a dream come true. Sometimes, when we are struggling most, we are most together."

These people, who say they "look down the road into the future together," have made their wishes come true with a journey which is both ended and just beginning. They carry within themselves the words of Isaiah,

If you remove from your midst oppression,
false accusation and malicious speech;
If you bestow your bread on the hungry
and satisfy the afflicted;
Then light shall rise for you in the darkness,
and the gloom shall become for you like
noonday (Is. 58:9-10).

St. Francis
Catholic Worker House

Cincinnati, Ohio

The sun is shining and the shadows well defined. The neighborhood is raggedy, in tatters, with large blowing trash and broken windows. The buildings, storefronts with apartments above, are of the substantial red brick which formed the base for early Cincinnati. The whispers of a gentler past can be heard. We are a few blocks from the sparkling, refurbished Fountain Square area, the Queen City's jewel. The area is called "Over The Rhine," and now is home to immigrants from Appalachia, people come north from Kentucky and West Virgina to try their luck.

Jim Mullen owned two bars in the area, then sold them both and went to tending bar. "That was when I began to hear the stories. People would tell me they had no place to sleep, no home. I'd say that I'd take them all home if I could but I didn't have the room."

A building became available to rent for $200.00 a month and Jim was forced to face his casual bartending promises. He rented, begged mattresses and the house was full. Jim had never heard of Dorothy Day and the Catholic Worker Movement. He thought he was doing something completely new, in 1983.

"I read an article in the paper about a Catholic Worker house in Washington, DC after I'd been doing this awhile. Well, I was impressed because they were doing everything I was doing and I hadn't even heard of them. So I wrote to the priest in charge and asked how I could join this Catholic Worker movement and he wrote back and said, 'Just put a sign on your door saying "Catholic Worker House" so I did. I've read a lot about Dorothy Day and the movement and I really admire her. We do our own thing but it is the same thing the others are doing, feeding people, putting them up."

"Originally it was simple. I went to work in the morning and when I came home at night I would unlock the doors and everyone would come in and stay the night. Then I realized the people had nothing to eat. I'm a good cook." (Laughter and teasing from others in the kitchen.) "I am! So I would make a big pot of soup everyday, then the word got out and soon there were lots of others coming around. Lots of hungry people."

The house is a look-alike to many others, peeling painted brick. The front door displays a difference, an ivitation, a large round emblem, cautiously tidy against the aging door. "As for me and my house, we will serve the Lord." Joshua 23:15. And it is through this door that 41,000 men, women and children passed last year in search of lunch. They pass under the plaster of paris smile of an enormous chipped St. Francis of Assisi and on the main room where tables are set, awaiting them. The hospitality of the house is gentle, nonchallenging. People eat what they are hungry for and then make room for others. The food is good, meaty, abundant, usually a stew served in a bowl. There is no feeling of stingyness, no uncertainty about whether there will be enough.

The kitchen is toward the back of the house and so small that it is a miracle that so many people could be fed from it. On the stove, a standard white enamel four burner, are three enormous pots full to the rim with pork and saurkraut, a smell evocative of the area's Germanic past. Volunteers move in and out of the cramped space, carrying bowls and bread and pots of coffee and water. It is almost 11:00 a.m., the hour that lunch begins.

Jim says, "After we had been in the house awhile we got the word from the landlord, 'Buy it or move.' We didn't have $15,000. In fact, we had $44 in the bank. I didn't know what to do. I wrote the editor of the *Catholic Telegraph Register* and asked her how people raise money. She didn't answer me, just put the letter in the paper. In the meantime, I started a novena to the Little Flower and supposedly if your prayer is going to be answered you will receive roses. Well, on the last day someone dropped off a box of used clothes and when I opened it there was a plastic rose on the top. I took it as a sign. The donations started coming and in another week I had $8,000. You feel pretty cocky with that kind of money in your pocket, so we started looking around and found this building (their current home) which had better possibilities so we bought it instead.

"Faith didn't make me start this community, I found faith in it. We started out with one refrigerator. Now we have seven freezers. I don't worry about food, there always seems to be enough. Sometimes it's really amazing. A woman called me and said she had some meat to give me, could we please come and pick it up. When we got there it was $5,000 worth of hotdogs and bacon and sausage, prepared meats. We came home with the van loaded and sat up half the night rearranging the freezers to fit in all the meat. What we couldn't stuff in we put in brown paper bags and went around the neighborhood giving it to people who could use it. Great gift."

"My greatest miracle? Something in me. Learning to have different expectations of other people. Learning they will do as much as they can. I think when someone gets drunk and stays drunk, 'Okay, he was sober for three weeks or five months, whatever, that's great, that's the best he can do.' No

disappointments, just acceptance. It's still hard sometimes."

Johnny Dean Barnes, slender to the point of leanness, handsome with deep rich eyes and the easy uncomplicated manner of country people, he is out of the mountains of Bluefield, West Virginia. "I was working for Odd Lots in Columbus and they laid me off, so I came to Cincinnati hoping they'd take me on. But I got real sick and ended up here. Then I been working here ever since, been about a month. I like it."

Johnny turns back to scrubbing the big pot in a blue bathtub immediately behind the kitchen which is reserved solely for cleaning the large equipment needed to feed so many.

Over his shoulder, "We were making beef stew last week. Had meat but no carrots or cabbage. The stew was all made but for the vegetables. An old man walked in carrying a bag of stuff from the free foodstore. He said, 'They gave me too much food over there.' Sure enough, when I opened the bag, in there was cabbage and carrots."

"Or the time we were getting ready to do our regular picnic in the park and were planning to have coleslaw, well the woman who said she'd bring mayonaise to make it didn't show up. Jim said we'd do without but just before we was going over to the park up pulls a van from a restaurant. Guess what? Tubs and tubs of coleslaw. Somebody's made too much."

A part of the miracle of St. Francis is the volunteers.

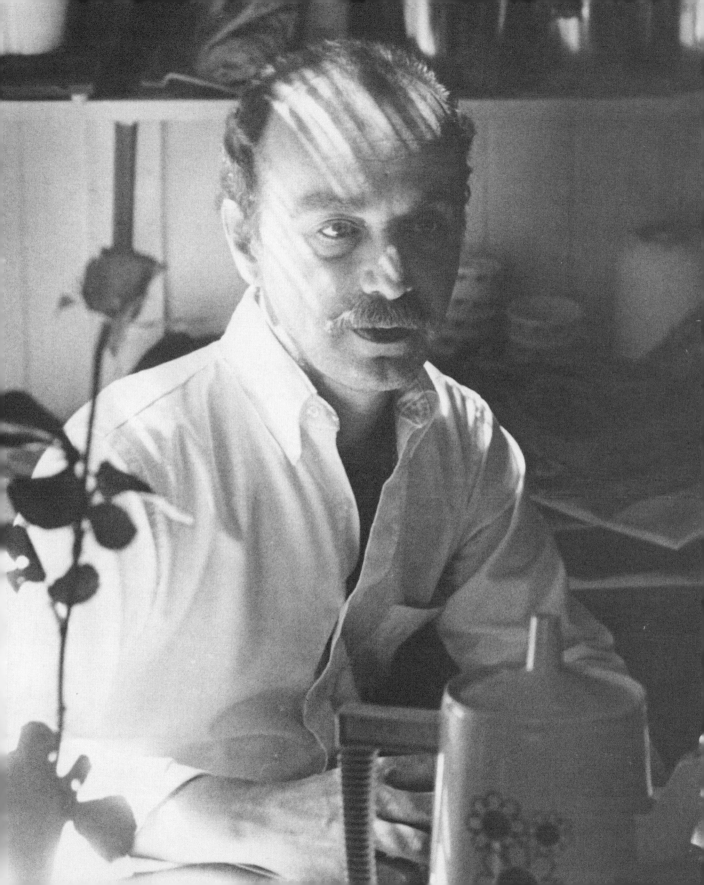

Alma Sullivan is a vivid grey-haired woman of independent thinking and comfortable proportions. She first arrived intending to do clerical work, after reading an article in the newspaper about the house. Though there is little paper to be processed in this place where needs are much more immediate, she has stayed to dish up and wipe tables and wash bowls and gather the guests to her heart. "There's one boy, he reminds me of my grandson in a way. But he just can't seem to get his life together. Oh, this boy did so well. He got off the drugs and back in school, even got a co-op job but he stopped taking his medicine and now he's right back where he was before. It's such a shame. I really worry about what's going to happen to him."

And then there is one enormous family, well known in the city, who discovered the house through their matriarch, a woman well into her seventies. She came, worked, saw need and called on those whom she knew best, her ten children, their spouses and children, some sixty strong. Now they not only staff the kitchen and prepare all the food every Sunday on a rotating basis, they also serve as insurance agent to the house, lawyer, van supplier and roofer.

There are miracles yet to happen. Jim remarks wistfully, "We want a farm. Not too far from the city. Maybe 35-40 minutes away, where we can grow our own vegetables and get some of the guests out in the fresh air for a while, where we can have liturgies. I don't know when it will be. Someone has made money available, enough for a good start. Maybe this year, maybe not. I have faith, I know it will come. I had this dream even before I heard of Peter Maurin.

"I used to worry about whether I had enough money to take a vacation. Now I really don't worry at all. Even though we aren't tax deductible, lots of people send us a check every month, just like he was one of our regular bills. One or two people send $50, others send $5 or $10. I just trust in God and there always seems to be enough.

Epilogue

The Catholic Worker Movement, which first saw daylight on the lower east side of New York during the direst months of the Great Depression, has ebbed and flowed with the needs of the times. In many ways, the 1980's find the movement stronger and more diverse than at any time in its 50-year history. Unfortunately, a cause of the strength is the need of the poor. Worker houses flower in pockets of poverty and sadness, in direct response to the call of the poor. It is an indictment of America in the 1980's that Catholic Worker Houses are so numerous and so busy. In some ways it would be wonderful if there were no houses, if everyone had a sheltered bed and full dinner table with no reason to line up in front of an inner-city house with a Catholic Worker sign on the door and wait for the dinner bell. Newspapers issuing from these houses continue to call for justice in hiring and in social services, and to request accountability in government for nuclear proliferation and for farming policies which drive the individual farmer from the land.

There have been two consistent threads in the history of the Catholic Worker movement: the meeting of a person's human needs (food, clothing, shelter), and resistance to government policies which robs workers of their stability in the workplace. Peter Maurin felt that the job of the Catholic Worker was to create order out of chaos; Dorothy Day called for "gentle personalism" which would allow people to live lives of free will and not of compulsion. In Catholic Worker houses across America volunteers work to create small islands of order in the midst of the anger and ugliness of the streets. Workers struggle to humanize the act of serving the poor even in such small ways as offering choices in bread, providing a table setting that is neat and attractive, and serving with good cheer. They strive to be mindful of the poor as people who, though they may be without in a material sense, are not faceless and without preferences.

It is not surprising that right from the beginning Dorothy faced obstacles of varying proportions. Some of the problems about which she spoke and wrote still plague the Catholic Worker today, problems such as volunteer recruitment and maintainence, and worker burnout. Volunteers are often so aware of and so overwhelmed by the naked need around them that they work, serve and listen to the point of mental and physical exhaustion. As one young laborer commented, "People here work until they drop, go off and regroup, then come back and work until they drop."

The burnout syndrome seems to be more pronounced in urban houses where the incessant beat of city life and struggle keeps the doorbell and the telephone ringing around the clock. The news is often not good: people drunk or beaten or robbed or ill, men without employment, women and children without shelter. One young woman spending her summer in a worker house observed, "It is a tide of misery, and no matter how hard we work we can't seem to stop the flow. People we helped last week are back today with more problems with no solutions. A woman came today. She's on probation now, and she has a 7-month-old baby girl. She had a fight with her mother, and her mother threw her out. I mean literally threw her out, threw her clothes and the baby's on the sidewalk. Now she's on the streets with a baby. On top of that, she's pregnant again and doesn't know how she's going to tell her husband, who's been in jail for the last year on bad check charges." The young volunteer's face sags, and she rests her face in her open palms.

Keeping volunteers in the face of such repeated misery is not quite as difficult as one might expect. Many urban worker houses seem to bulge with willing workers, men and women eager to come once a week or once a month to cook, peel and freeze, to sort clothes and answer the door. The reasons are the same, house after house, city after city:

"I really feel Jesus present here."

"I came to know what the Eucharist means here."

"I'm not a Catholic, in fact, I'm Jewish, but I have been coming here on the Tuesday shift for two years. There is this experience of joy; you can almost touch it."

"This house, this meal, helps me to remember that I am very like the people coming to eat. I'm broken; I have faults. At the moment I happen to be well-employed, but it is good for me to remember how close I, and you, are to being on the other side of the counter."

"When I first came here I was scared and the smell bothered me, you know, wood smoke in the winter and sweat in the summer. Now I know a lot of the regulars and they know me. I can really say that they are friends, and they miss me if I don't show up."

Rural communities seem to suffer from the opposite problem—a lack of enduring volunteers. Perhaps this is due to the isolation, their choice to dwell outside of the mainstream. Or perhaps disillusionment with the demanding nature of farm work sends the inexperienced volunteer back to the city.

The work on the farms is hard, grueling. Since many of the farms choose to be organic, willing friends find themselves hour after hour in the potato patch picking potato bugs or pulling weeds by hand. In winter houses which are unwilling to use gas and electric utilities may lack adequate heat. Since most farm workers must live on the farm, the charm pales quickly unless one is a hearty determined sort.

Yet one of the gifts which the Catholic Worker has to offer is a return to the land and to what the land means. For the worker, it means the willingness to acknowledge the flow of seasons, the genuine dignity of the soil which will produce in season what it can, the reality of pests, the cost of heat early or frost late. There is none of the attitude of the 1980's farmer who will force nature into submission, regardless of the cost. The Catholic Worker farms live in poverty, eating no strawberries out of season, putting no land in the federal land bank. They live on beans this week and broccoli the next, all the while providing produce to the nearest soup kitchen. This is a hard life, and while many are attracted back to the land by some romantic notion of bucolic bliss, few stay on to harvest the crops.

With all these struggles, the Catholic Worker Movement has much to offer the world today, namely, the experience of life-giving poverty, faith-filled service and self-less love. In this regard, it is indeed counter to the prevailing culture of the West.

The Catholic Worker offers poverty, but not destitution, as an ideal. As Dorothy Day wrote:

Love of brother means voluntary poverty, stripping one's self, etc. It also means non-participation in those comforts and luxuries which have been manufactured by the exploitation of others.... While our brothers suffer, from lack of necessities, we will refuse to enjoy comforts.... And we must keep this vision in mind, recognize the truth of it, the necessity for it, even though we do not, cannot, live up to it (*Meditations*, p. 58).

Therefore workers cover themselves with clothing from the donations, as do their guests, eat what is given and "vacation" in the war zones of Nicaragua. One long-termer commented, somewhat wryly, "I wouldn't dare show up at dinner in new clothes." It is poverty chosen intentionally. One of its joys is the return to pleasure in little things—an ice cream cone, a bottle of wine. Their very rarity returns them to the category of treats. The lack of a large number of expensive personal possessions permits the freedom to not worry about them, to not need to protect them. Voluntary poverty frees the conscience.

The issue of this poverty becomes less painful when we look to the truly poor, those who suffer a destitition which grinds them down, depriving them of even the most basic of human rights: to shelter, to food, to decent coverings. Though most Worker houses do not have the means to significantly alter the circumstances of their guests, they *can* give a willing ear to their stories, a recognition of their humanity. In sharing conversation, jokes, sorrows, the common pot, dignity is given to the individual person, an experience often lacking in the world of food-stamp lines and welfare offices.

Though the Catholic Worker Movement has often been criticized as a bandaid for a problem which calls for radical surgery, it is interesting that many house staff members work outside the house in jobs which help to heal the community in other ways. One is a Legal Aid lawyer, another teaches illiterates, a third is a minister in a nursing home, yet another runs a day-care service for young children of Hispanic mothers who are learning English and developing job skills. It can be a more than challenging life!

Every urban house benefits if it has one staff member who can commit to being the full-time housekeeper, door-answerer and telephone person, and no house could survive without those people who willingly give an afternoon or evening or two a month. They come as individuals, as part of youth groups, as members of local parishes of various denominations. These groups settle after several months of commitment to a core of regulars, as those who find the place uncomfortable or challenging to their own life-styles fade away.

There are other ways in which to contribute. Some people give up a specific pleasure in order to support the efforts of a particular house. Checks arrive in the mail, many of them surprises, just at the moment when there are no more funds. Houses which have no "walking-around" money have buildings donated to them. A letter from Michael Kirwan brings this information:

This week we are busily moving furniture, household articles, curtains and such into our new house of hospitality for elderly homeless women.

In June I saw a house just down the street advertised in the *Washington Post* for $120,000. A beautiful restored Victorian townhouse. I immediately signed the contract to buy even though I had no money whatsoever. Through some wonderful friends in Virginia, we raised 50,000 and I took out a loan for 70,000. So we are moving in this week. It will accommodate five women to begin with...

The Kansas City house has this experience: "We've never ever made an appeal for money, but we always have enough." This seems to be a recognition by many of the value of the work, of the honesty of the workers, of the fact that they carry a goodly portion of the cross.

The Catholic Worker is sometimes criticized for a certain lack of organization, a criticism well-justified in some houses. In these places, both at first and at second glance, chaos is visible everywhere, especially near mealtimes, or when all the crops bear fruit at once. Some volunteers are repulsed by the lack of structure, even many who have previously worked among the poor. But many houses show a pride in the firm reliance on "Christian anarchy." While no official definition exists, the term has come to mean the absence of a governing structure, permitting each individual to follow his or her inner call from God to be of service. In practice one finds that the person who chooses to do the books may also volunteer to go to the food bank and might be found scrubbing toilets after dinner. One who seems to be in charge on a given day is discovered performing the simplest of tasks on the next. Those who are by inclination order-givers may quickly find that there are no order-takers. Catholic Worker houses have become a safe haven for both compulsive workaholics and chronic non-doers. The early worker farms were especially plagued by the latter. Today, many houses practice consensual decision-making, and all hopefully will bear the burdens of labor evenly, though none is forced. There is no boss, only the call of God, to bring forth one's efforts.

Dorothy Day was often irritated by those willing ones who would come to her and say, "Tell me what to do." She would flatly respond, "Look around you; see what needs doing. I cannot tell you."

As Catholic Worker volunteers are divided in labor, so they are divided in politics. There is a long political tradition in the Catholic Worker press of taking up unpopular causes and pursuing them even when it means the loss of friends. Notable among these causes was the Worker's pacifist stand during World War II. This is what Dorothy Day said:

Dear Fellow Workers in Christ: Lord God, merciful God, our Father, shall we keep silent or shall we speak? And if we speak, what shall we say?... We will print the words of Christ, who is with us always, even to the end of the World. 'Love your enemies, do good to those who hate you, and pray for those who persecute and calumniate you....' Because of our refusal to assist in the prosecution of war and our insistance that our collaboration be one for peace, we may find ourselves in difficulties. But we trust in the generosity and understanding of our friends and of our government, to permit us to continue to use our paper to 'preach' Christ crucified' (*The Catholic Worker*, January, 1942).

There has been also a consistent alignment with the rights of the laborer which has led some to identify the paper with Communism, though it quotes Jesus and the popes. There is the public refusal to pay taxes and, in the early '60s, a positive response to the efforts of Fidel Castro's government in the areas of education, health and housing. And perhaps the best-known photograph of Dorothy Day is one taken during the United Farm Workers' strike: an old lady, on strike, looking up into the face of a big policeman. She went to jail.

Peter Maurin's *Easy Essays* is a revolutionary's guidebook. Printed and reprinted, these short teachings preach radical Christianity. Radical in the '30s, radical now. With such forebears, it is not surprising that many on the staff of Catholic Worker houses picket the Pentagon, resist United States policy in Central America, and protest the diversion of taxes to the war machine instead of to those in need. They keep vigil at the railroad crossings where nuclear "white trains" pass. They put themselves forward for arrest at White Sands and at Rocky Flats. The first young man to burn his draft card was a Catholic Worker.

A lead article by Tim Lambert in the May 1987 issue of *The Catholic Worker* comments:

The Catholic Worker of 1933 is filled with labor news, strikes and organizing, statements of support and demands. With the Second World War comes reporting of the devastation in Europe and the right to conscientious objection at home. A theology of peace is outlined, as an antidote to the years of bloodshed. The 1950s and 1960s bring news of the civil rights struggle, and resistance to the cold war, turned hot in Korea and Vietnam. In the pages of the 1970s one finds news of the United Farm Worker efforts to organize.

And today? The last few years have found us writing of nuclear armaments, and United States intervention in Central America. We look back on these years and find again a time of war, and preparations for war.

So much writing on war and peace. There is something amazing in it, because we have little to say. We are pacifists. We do not believe that one can take the life of another, or even plan to do so, and it not be a sin.

When asked about particular weapons systems or arms negotiations, we can only recommend a unilateral disarmament. This often stirs a scandal, and especially when we are passing out leaflets or demonstrating for peace, we are dismissed as foolish, or as agents of Soviet propaganda, or simply as naive. How could it be otherwise today, in this, the most heavily armed nation the world has ever known? At most, we feel we are scattering seeds, the smallest of seeds, with our words....

We ask why the whole Church has not followed us to proclaim this message, but know, ourselves, that it is because we are still found to be naive, and have so little to say to the "real" world.

Those "little seeds" sown can even cause dissension in Worker Houses themselves. In some houses today the question of homosexuality and the crisis of AIDS has brought division. The prayer is that by discernment of God's Will, peace will be made, and wounds healed.

With their commitment to feed the hungry, clothe the naked, shelter the homeless and bring peace, what do these people, scattered on farms and in ghettoes, have to offer to church, to community? Perhaps the outstanding gift is their daily witness to the gospel of Jesus Christ. This is not a gift of a dramatic single witness, but rather the unpublicized constant witness of continuing service. Christian service programs in high schools and adult programs of Christian initiation have, in many cities, come to incorporate frequent working visits as a normal part of their routines. Exposed to the often joyful experience of people working together for others, and for themselves, visitors would be hard-pressed to see this radical living of the Christian call as a dreadful or dismal experience. Whether these people return or not, they have hopefully encountered Jesus present in the washing of the dishes and the serving of the beans, in the laughter and tears of the guests. Perhaps they have been fortunate enough to have met Christ in the eyes of everyone to whom they handed a full and delicious plate. As Dorothy once said, "We can only give what we have, in the name of Jesus. Thank God for directing our vocation. We did not choose this work. He sent it to us (*By Little and By Little*, Robert Ellsberg, p. 112).

Appendix: Catholic Worker Houses

Alabama

BREAD AND ROSES HOUSE OF
HOSPITALITY
5325 GEORGIA
BIRMINGHAM, AL 35212

(205) 595-6399

Hospitality for women and children; employment and housing help; medical help; newsletter

Arizona

CASA MARIA
401 E. 26 St.
TUCSON, AR 85713

(602) 624-0312

Soup kitchen daily; men's hospitality, clothing, peace and justice work: Eucharist on Monday

California

CASA DE CLARA
318 N 6th St.
SAN JOSE, CA 95112

(408) 297-8330

Hospitality for women and children; food; clothes

CATHOLIC WORKER FARM
PO BOX 53
SHEEPRANCH, CA 95250

(209) 728-2193

Meetings and retreats; local women's crisis work; work with developmentally disabled adults during summer; struggling to establish a candle business; newsletter, *Earth Abides*

MARTIN DE PORRES HOUSE OF
HOSPITALITY
225 POTRERO
SAN FRANCISCO, CA 94110

(415) 552-0240

Two meals daily; clothing; showers; newsletter, *Gentle Personalism*

ORANGE COUNTY CATHOLIC
WORKER
311 S. MAIN ST.
SANTA ANA, CA 92701

(714) 835-6304

Hospitality for men and women; meal in family setting for small group; Eucharist; peace and justice work

FRANCISCAN WORKERS OF JUNIPERO
SERRA
715 JEFFERSON
SALINAS, CA 93905

(408) 424-1102

Soup kitchen, "Dorothy's Place"; labor camp visitation; clothing; religious instruction for children; peace and justice work; round table discussion; Eucharist

PETER MAURIN CATHOLIC WORKER
PO BOX 8267
2232 ISLAND AVE
SAN DIEGO, CA 92102

(619) 231-8020

Hospitality to women with young children; clothing; emergency campground; newsletter, *The Catholic Witness*

SACRAMENTO CATHOLIC WORKER
619 12th ST.
SACRAMENTO, CA 95814

(916) 447-3758

Hospitality for AIDS patients; anti-nuclear resistance

CATHOLIC WORKER HOUSE
545 CASSIA ST.
REDWOOD CITY, CA 94063

(415) 366-4415

Sanctuary to troubled teens, battered infants and people from Central America; food program

OAKLAND CATHOLIC WORKER
4848 E 14th St.
OAKLAND, CA 94601

(415) 533-7375

Limited hospitality; low-cost produce store; resistance work; volunteers needed

SAN DIEGO CATHOLIC WORKER
3159 IMPERIAL AVENUE
PO BOX 40168
SAN DIEGO, CA 92104

(619) 233-0519

Men's hospitality—30 to 60 days; volunteers needed

AMMON HENNACY CATHOLIC WORKER
632 N. BRITTANIA ST.
LOS ANGELES, CA 90003

(213) 267-8789

HOSPITALITY KITCHEN
PO BOX 21471
821 E 6th St.
LOS ANGELES, CA 90021

(213) 972-9656

ZEDEKAH HOUSE

(213) 626-9087

Limited hospitality; daily public meal; free medical clinic; newspaper, *The Catholic Agitator*

SANTA ROSA CATHOLIC WORKER
PO BOX 3364 (95402)
110 ROBERTS AVENUE
SANTA ROSA, CA 95401

(707) 575-8342

Food pantry; clothing; newsletter; peacework

Colorado

DENVER CATHOLIC WORKER
2420 WELTON
DENVER, COLORADO 80205

(303) 296-6390

Long-term hospitality for men, women, families; worship on Wednesday; clarification of thought on Friday; woodworking shop for toys and coffins; second house for transitional housing; garden in rural area

Connecticut

DOROTHY DAY HOSPITALITY HOUSE
PO BOX 922
11 SPRING ST.
DANBURY, CT 06810

(203) 792-7494

Hospitality; meal daily

GUADALUPE HOUSE
PO BOX 1343
79 BEACON ST
WATERBURY, CT 06721

(203) 753-5676

Hospitality for men and women; soup kitchen daily; clarification of thought one Friday a month.

Washington, DC

OLIVE BRANCE
1322 KENYON ST NW
WASHINGTON, DC 20008

(202) 332-6247

Peace and justice work; soup kitchen; prayer presence at the Pentagon

ST. FRANCIS CATHOLIC WORKER
1115 6TH ST NW
WASHINGTON, DC 20001

(202) 628-1365

Hospitality to men and women

DOROTHY DAY HOUSE
503 ROCK CREEK CHURCH RD, NW
WASHINGTON, DC 20010

(202) 829-0340

Hospitality for families with children; support for Zacchaeus soup kitchen; peace and justice work; newsletter, *The Little Way;* volunteers needed

MARY HARRIS CATHOLIC WORKER
939 T STREET NW
WASHINGTON, DC 20001

(202) 265-0170

House of hospitality for elderly women; dinner daily; Eucharist

LLEWELLYN   SCOTT   CATHOLIC
WORKER HOUSE
1305 T STREET NW
WASHINGTON, DC 20009

(202) 332-9675

Home for men; evening meal; food carried to grates around State Department nightly; drop-in-center; Eucharist on Wednesday; volunteers needed

STELLA MARIS CATHOLIC WORKER
1801 E. BROAD ST.
SAVANNAH, GA 31401

(912) 232-4342

Long-term hospitality for men; peace and justice work; clarification of thought once a month; Eucharist Monday, Wednesday, Friday; newsletter, *Stella Maris*

ANAWIM HOUSE
509 N GENESEE ST.
WAUKEGAN, IL 60085

(312) 662-3990

Permanent hospitality for retarded young people

DOROTHY DAY CATHOLIC WORKER
HOUSE
901 20TH ST.
ROCK ISLAND, IL 61201

(309) 786-1737

Hospitality for women and families; resistance against the Rock Island Arsenal; newsletter, *The Catholic Activist*

ST. FRANCIS OF ASSISI HOUSE
4652 N. KENMORE
CHICAGO, IL 60640

(312) 561-5073

Hospitality; newsletter, *Chicago Catholic Worker*

ST ELIZABETH CATHOLIC WORKER
8025 S. HONORE
Chicago, IL 60620

(312) 874-2500

Hospitality for all; food pantry and clothing room; meals for the neighborhood; occasional newsletter; peace and justice work

Iowa

SIOUX CITY CATHOLIC WORKER
HOUSE
1110 10th ST.
SIOUX CITY, IA 51105

(712) 255-6113

Hospitality for women and children; groceries; soup/sandwich supper three nights; peace and justice work; newsletter, *The Pilgrim*

ST. FRANCIS CATHOLIC WORKER
PO BOX 1533
321 E. 8th ST
WATERLOO, IA 20703

(319) 232-2116

Hospitality for men, women, families; dinner daily; groceries; newsletter, *St. Francis Catholic Worker*

DOROTHY DAY COMMUNITY FARM
RR 1 BOX 40
WILLIAMSBURG, IA 52361

(319) 668-2786

Produce grown for Cedar Rapids and Des Moines Catholic Workers, and Kindred soup kitchen; space for workers' retreats

CASA CANCION DE MARIA CATHOLIC
WORKER
382 E 21ST.
DUBUQUE, IA 52001

(319) 583-2043

Hospitality for families and women; peace and justice work; clothing; groceries; newsletter; Friday round-table discussions

CATHOLIC WORKER HOUSE OF
HOSPITALITY
2733 AVENUE N
FORT MADISON, IA 52627

(319) 372-3983

Hospitality for families of prisoners, women and children; outreach to elderly; distribution of food and clothes; round- table discussions; newsletter, *The Dove;* volunters needed

DES MOINES CATHOLIC WORKER
PO BOX 4551
DES MOINES, IA 50306

LAZARUS HOSPITALITY HOUSE
1317 8th St.
DESMOINES, IA 50314

(515) 243-0765

Hospitality for women and families; groceries; peace and justice work; newsletter *Via Pacis*

Kansas

SHALOM CATHOLIC WORKER HOUSE
2100 N. 13TH ST.
KANSAS CITY, KS 66104

(913) 321-2206

Hospitality for men; peace-education center and library; Friday night clarification of thought; Eucharist on Sunday; newspaper, *Shalom News;* teachers' paper, *Olive Branch*

ST. JOHN OF THE CROSS CATHOLIC WORKER
1027 5TH AVENUE SE
CEDAR RAPIDS, IA 52403

(319) 362-9041

Noon meal daily; shelter for women and families; peace and justice work; newsletter, *The Dark Night*

DAVENPORT CATHOLIC WORKER
PO BOX 3813
806 W. 5TH ST. DAVENPORT, IA 52802

(319) 324-8431

Short-term hospitality for men; meal daily; resistance work; newspaper, *Rock Island-Davenport Catholic Radical;* volunteers needed.

Kansas

ST. FRANCIS CATHOLIC WORKER HOUSE
PO BOX 465
618 N. ADAMS
JUNCTION CITY, KS 66441

(913) 238-5838

Hospitality for men; clothing

EMMAUS HOUSE
802 N. 5TH
GARDEN CITY, KS 67846

(316) 275-2008

Hospitality for men and families; two meals a day; groceries; workers needed

Maryland

VIVA HOUSE
26 S. MOUNT ST.
BALTIMORE, MD 21223

(301) 233-2049

Hospitality for homeless women; food distribution; newsletter, *Enthusiasm*

Massachusetts

NOONDAY FARM
BOX 71
WINCHENDON SPRINGS, MA 01477

(617) 297-3226

Organic vegetable garden supplies food to soup kitchens in Boston area; limited hospitality for soup-kitchen guests; resistance work; ministry of music; long-term shelter

THE MUSTARD SEED
93 PIEDMONT ST.
WORCESTER, MA 01609

(617) 754-7098

9 MERRICK ST 01609
Worcester, MA 01609

(617) 756-3397

Meals at Piedmont St. daily; Friday night meetings; hospitality at Merrick St.

ST. FRANCIS AND THERESE
CATHOLIC WORKER
52 MASON
WORCESTER, MA 01610

(617) 753-3588

Hospitality for all; peace and justice work; clarification of thought every other Wednesday; morning and evening prayer; newspaper, *The Catholic Radical*

Michigan

DAY HOUSE
2640 TRUMBULL
DETROIT, MI 48216

(313) 963-4539

Hospitality for women and children; soup kitchen, Manna Community Meal, resistance, newspaper, *On The Edge*

OBONAUDSAWIN FARM
4218 BABCOCK RD.
LEXINGTON, MI 48450

(313) 359-5295

Organic farming, produce shared with soup kitchen; limited hospitality; volunteers needed

Massachusetts

HALEY HOUSE
23 DARTMOUTH ST.
BOSTON, MA 02116

(617) 262-2940

Soup kitchen for men mornings; dinner for elderly four days; drop-in storefront; nuclear weapons resistance; weekly vigil worship; newsletter; volunteers needed

Minnesota

ST. JOSEPH HOUSE
2101 PORTLAND AVENUE
MINNEAPOLIS, MN 55404

(612) 874-8867

Hospitality for women and children; drop-in center four days; clothing; groceries; peace and justice work; newsletter, *House News*

DOROTHY DAY HOSPITALITY HOUSE
420 5TH AVENUE SW
ROCHESTER, MN

MAILING ADDRESS: ASSISI HEIGHTS
PO BOX 4900
ROCHESTER, MN 55903

Hospitality; peace work; quarterly publication, *Dorothy Day Hospitality House*

JEAN DONOVAN CATHOLIC WORKER
611 S. 8TH AVENUE
ST. CLOUD, MN 56301

(612) 252-1018

Hospitality for men, women, families; peace and justice work

DOROTHY DAY HOUSE OF
HOSPITALITY
714 8TH ST. S
MOORHEAD, MN 56560

(218) 233-5763

Missouri

HOLY FAMILY HOUSE
908 E. 31ST.
KANSAS CITY, MO 64109

(816) 753-2677

Dinner six days; hospitality for women and families; food distribution; peace and justice work; newsletter; Eucharist on Thursday

ELLA DIXON HOUSE
1540 N. 17TH ST.
ST. LOUIS, MO 63106

(314) 231-2039

Long-term hospitality; peace and justice work; liturgy one day a week; newsletter, *The Round Table*

KAREN HOUSE
1840 HOGAN
ST. LOUIS, MO 63106

(314) 621-4052

Shelter for women with children; clothes and food distribution; peace and justice; liturgy one day a week; volunteers needed

New York

MARYHOUSE
55 E. 3RD ST.
NEW YORK, NY 10003

(212) 777-9617

Hospitality for women; breakfast and lunch for women and children; food distribution; clothing for women and children; showers; peace and justice work; nightly vespers, Eucharist; newspaper, *The Catholic Worker*

New Jersey

LEAVENHOUSE
644 STATE ST.
CAMDEN, NJ 08102

(609) 966-4596

Lunch six days; community organizing; advocacy for the homeless; monthly education meetings; annual newsletter, *Leavenhouse*

Nevada

ST. JOHN THE BAPTIST HOUSE
1309 GOLD AVENUE
LAS VEGAS, NV 89106

(702) 647-0728

Hospitality; food carried to the streets six days; dinner Thursday; vigil at Federal Building six days; newsletter, *Manna in the Wilderness*

New York

PETER MAURIN FARM
RD 1 PO BOX 80
MARLBORO, NY 12542

(914) 236-4774

Organic gardening, produce to city houses; community living

DOROTHY DAY HOUSE
c/o CATHEDRAL
259 E. ONONDAGA ST.
SYRACUSE, NY 13202

(315) 476-0617

Short-term hospitality for women and children (boys 10 and under); newsletter, *Dorothy Day House*

ST. JOSEPH HOUSE
36 E. 1ST ST.
NEW YORK, NY 10003

(212) 254-1640

Hospitality for men; soupline Wednesday, Thursday and Sunday; clothes; help with welfare problems and housing; Eucharist; Friday night discussions here or at Mary house; peace and justice work; newspaper, *The Catholic Worker;* nightly vespers

BETHANY HOUSE
169 ST BRIDGET'S DRIVE
ROCHESTER, NY 14605

(716) 454-4197

Hospitality for woean and children; Newspaper, *Agape*

UNITY KITCHEN COMMUNITY
PO BOX 650
385 W. ONONDAGA ST.
SYRACUSE, NY 13202

(315) 478-5552

Sit-down meal for small number of guests each night; newsletter, *The Unity Grapevine*

ZACCHAEUS HOUSE
89 PINE ST.
BINGHAMTON, NY 13901

(607) 773-0246

Christ-room hospitality for women with children; peace and justice work; newsletter, *Zacchaeus House*

UNITY ACRES
PO BOX 153
COUNTY ROAD 2
ORWELL, NY 13426

(315) 298-6215

Permanent hospitality for over 100 men; newsletter, *Unity Acres Newsletter*

MARANATHA HOUSE
PO BOX 73 BRIDGE STATION
2115 10TH ST.
NIAGARA FALLS, NY 14305

(716) 284-6054

Hospitality for men; work with The Lampstead soup kitchen daily; clothing

ST. JOSEPH'S HOUSE OF HOSPITALITY
PO BOX 1062
402 SOUTH AVENUE
ROCHESTER, NY 14603

(716) 232-3262

Hospitality for men, November through mid-April; clothing; lunch daily; newspaper, *Rochester Catholic Worker*

ARTHUR SHEEHAN HOUSE
314 4TH ST.
BROOKLYN, NY 11215

(718) 788-1425

Hospitality; work with soup kitchen; monthly round-table discussions

Ohio

ST. FRANCIS CATHOLIC WORKER HOUSE
1437 WALNUT ST.
CINCINNATI, OH 45210

(513) 241-7211

Hospitality for men and families; soup kitchen daily, October to May; picnic in the park Thursdays through the summer; interim housing for male jail inmates waiting for alchohol/drug treatment centers newsletter; *Walnut Street Journal*

ST. FRANCIS CATHOLIC WORKER HOUSE
877 E. 150TH
CLEVELAND, OH 44110

(216) 249-6131

Hospitality for men

JEAN DONOVAN CATHOLIC WORKER
HOUSE
1075 E. 72ND ST.
CLEVELAND, OH 44103

(216) 431-0367

Hospitality for women and children

DOROTHY DAY HOUSE—WEST
3008 CLINTON AVENUE
CLEVELAND, OH 44113

Hospitality; food and clothes distribution

DOROTHY DAY HOUSE—EAST
14509 DARLEY
CLEVELAND, OH 44110

Hospitality for families

CLEVELAND CATHOLIC WORKER
COMMUNITY
4241 LORAIN AVENUE
CLEVELAND, OH 44113

(216) 281-6854

Hospitality for men; Friday night clarification
of thought

ST. HERMAN'S MONASTERY/ HOUSE
OF HOSPITALITY
4410 FRANKLIN BLVD.
CLEVELAND, OH 44113

(216) 961-3806

Hospitality for men; drop-in center serving
three meals daily; sanctuary; newsletter

STANLEY ROTHER HOUSE
78 N. OLYMPIA
TULSA, OK 74127

(918) 583-4402

Hospitality for all; meals; food and clothing
distribution; newsletter, *The Eye of the Storm*

Oregon

ROUND TABLE HOUSE
5252 NE 17TH ST.
PORTLAND, OR 97211

(503) 288-1888

Christ-room hospitality; meals

Pennsylvania

ST. CLARE HOUSE
2858 KENSINGTON AVENUE
PHILADELPHIA, PA 19133

Hospitality for women

PHILADELPHIA CATHOLIC WORKER
430 W. JEFFERSON
PHILADELPHIA, PA 19122

(215) 232-7823

Hospitality; neighborhood involvement

ST. JOSEPH HOUSE
2436 N. FRONT ST.
PHILADELPHIA, PA 19133

(215) 423-9848

Hospitality for men; showers; laundry; coun-
selling

DUNCAN AND PORTER HOUSE OF
HOSPITALITY AND RESISTANCE
1332 SHEFFIELD ST.
PITTSBURGH, PA 15233

(412) 231-2766

Hospitality for men; newsletter

Rhode Island

AMOS HOUSE
PO BOX 2873
415 FRIENDSHIP ST.
PROVIDENCE, RI 02907

(401) 272-0220

Hospitality for men and women; breakfast and lunch six days; clothing; volunteers needed

Texas

CASA JUAN DIEGO
PO BOX 70113
4814 ROSE
HOUSTON, TX 77270

(713) 869-7376

Hospitality and transportation for refugees from Central America and Mexico; soup kitchen; food; clothing; medical and legal services; English classes; Spanish /English newspaper; Eucharist weekly

JONAH HOUSE
1011 HUTCHINS ROAD
DALLAS, TX. 75203

(214) 941-6558

Hospitality for women, women with children, families; meals for neighborhood people; rent, clothing and food assistance; round table discussion; occasional liturgy; newsletter, *Jonah's Wail*

SAN ANTONIO CATHOLIC WORKER
622 NOLAN ST.
SAN ANOTONIO, TX 78202

(512) 224-2932

Hospitality for families; soup kitchen M-F; peace and justice work, focus on Central America; Tuesday prayer; round table discussion; monthly newsletter

CATHOLIC WORKER PILGRIM HOUSE
PO BOX 11411
LUBBOCK, TX 79408

(806) 797-0916

Washington

EMMANUEL HOUSE
PO BOX 223
133 SUNSET
PAULSBO, WA 98370

(206) 697-1731

Christ-room; drop-in center; lunches for school children packed; food; peace and justice; pregnancy counseling; occasional liturgy

BREAD AND ROSES CATHOLIC WORKER
PO BOX 2699
1320 E. 8TH
OLYMPIA, WA 98507

Hospitality for women and children; two daily meals; peace and justice work; sanctuary help

PACEM IN TERRIS
331 17TH EAST
SEATTLE, WA 98112

(206) 322-2447

Meal for women, children, families, elderly Monday to Friday

West Virginia

TYRA DUNN CATHOLIC WORKER FARM
BOX 49A HC 73
ALDERSON, WV

Working farm for women's hospitality; permanent housing; volunteers needed

CATHOLIC WORKER FARM
RTE 1
PO BOX 413
WEST HAMLIN, WV 25571

(304) 824-7249

Farm demonstrates decentralist economy using principles of Peter Maurin and Catholic Worker Movement; raises dairy goats and chickens

OSCAR ROMERO CATHOLIC WORKER HOUSE OF HOSPITALITY
PO BOX 942
400 FOREST AVENUE
MORGANTOWN, WV 26505

(304) 291-1418

Hospitality to families, especially those who come to the Appalachian Regional Hospital for treatment; outreach to people in the surrounding mountain region; newsletter, *Beatitudes*

JOHN FILLIGAR CATHOLIC WORKER FARM
48 FHC 73
ALDERSON, WV 24910

(304) 445-7143

Permanent hospitality to men from the streets of Washington , DC; volunteers needed

ALDERSON HOSPITALITY HOUSE
BOX 579
203 HIGH ST.
ALDERSON, WV 24910

(304) 445-2980

Hospitality; transportation for visitors to Federal Women's Prison; newsletter, *Judgment*

Wisconsin

CASA MARIA CATHOLIC WORKER HOUSE
PO BOX 05206
1131 N. 21ST.
MILWAUKEE, WI 53205

(414) 344-5745

Hospitality for families and women; food; clothes; used furniture for families; showers; sanctuary; war resistance; newsletter

CATHOLIC WORKER ARCHIVES
MARQUETTE UNIVERSITY
1415 W. WISCONSON AVE.
MILWAUKEE, WI, 53233